Fellowship
is Life

Lack of Fellow
ship is Death

SOCIALISM·THE·HOPE·OF·THE·WORLD

FELLOWSHIP IS LIFE

The Story of the
Clarion Cycling Club

DENIS PYE

CLARION
Publishing

First published 1995 by Clarion Publishing
34 Temple Road, Halliwell,
Bolton BL1 3LT, Lancashire, England

Reprinted 1996
New edition 2004

British Library Cataloguing in Publication Data
A catalogue record for this book
is available from the British Library

ISBN 0 9525071 1 0

Typeset and designed by
Andi Chapple Design, Sedbergh
andichapple@onetel.net.uk

Printed by
The Cromwell Press, Trowbridge

Illustrations in Text

	page
Humber Safety Bicycle of 1892	1
Design by William Morris for a Democratic Federation membership card	2
Front page of *The Clarion*'s first issue, December 1891	7
Joe Waddington ('Clarion Joe')	8
Easter Meet programme, Chester 1898	22
Heading in Blatchford's *Merrie England*, first (shilling) edition	27
Mr and Mrs Bennett, stewards at the first (Bucklow Hill) clubhouse	35
Enid Stacy addresses a Van meeting, 1898	40
Clarion Van postcard, 1907	41
Valley House, Styal, last of the Cheshire clubhouses	61
Cartoon in the unofficial *Clarion Cyclist* magazine, 1930	71

Note: The title page and back cover contain Walter Crane's letterhead design for the National Clarion Cycling Club

PREFACE

In 1944, to mark the fiftieth anniversary of the formation of the first Clarion Cycling Club in Birmingham, the National Clarion published a Jubilee Souvenir. It consisted of ten pages of text and photographs, plus six pages of advertisements – and it sold for sixpence. Most of it was written by Tom Groom, who had chaired the very first meeting of the Birmingham club. (He was still, in 1944, Life President of the national organisation – an honour bestowed on him in 1930.) A short introduction was contributed by Ernest Sugden, National Secretary since 1921, and the booklet was edited by the Racing Secretary, Alex Taylor, who wrote on the final page:

> Some day, someone will write the history of the Clarion Cycling Club. Some generous spirit will get down to the painstaking task of research among the old minute books, through the files of old *Clarions*, *Cyclings* and other journals; will accept reports from local sections and stories from old members. He will compose the selection in so many pages and then we shall be able to say that the official history of the club has been written.

The little booklet, produced under war-time paper restrictions, remained for another fifty years the only published history of the Clarion. Mine is not claimed to be the 'official' version; merely another attempt to put together a history of the Club of which I have been a member for not much more than a decade. My research has been far from exhaustive, though it started before I actually joined the Clarion.

Twelve years ago, proud of our new tandem, my wife Wendy and I got talking to an 'old-timer', Frank Harwood, who had noticed the machine parked in Bolton's town-hall square while we did some shopping. He reminisced about the good times he had enjoyed with Bolton Clarion Cycling Club in the 1920s. He told us that the Club still existed – in the form, we later discovered, of five or six other old-timers who had been holding only an Annual Meeting for the previous ten years. Frank invited us to visit him for a cup of tea at his flat, where he gave us two treasured Clarion mementoes: a national membership card and a handbook, both dated 1929. (Later, he also parted with his precious silver badge.) This chance meeting was the inspiration for us to seek out the Bolton Clarion Secretary. We joined to help revive the Club, and I began to research its history.

I want to acknowledge the help given me by Frank Harwood, the late Sid Clemmett, who was Bolton Section's Secretary from 1935 to 1947 and again from 1973 to 1983, Jack Mullineux, Albert Winstanley, and many others over the years. I cannot mention them all by name, but they include: Derek Roberts of the Fellowship of Cycling Old-Timers, Stephen Bird and Andy Flinn of the National Museum of Labour History's Archive Centre, staff at Manchester Central Library and the Working-Class Movement Library in Salford, and Ian Ingham. My thanks to these, and to all the other friends and comrades who have freely given their assistance, encouragement and inspiration – especially my tandem-partner, Wendy.

Denis Pye
Bolton, Lancashire
January 1995

NOTE TO 2004 EDITION

Since this book was first published the Clarion Cycling Club has emerged intact into the 21st century, although there have been two changes of National Secretary in the intervening years. Annual Meets have taken place every Easter, just as they have since 1895, albeit with declining attendances. New sections have been formed, notably at Oakhill College, Whalley, in Lancashire, but also in Herefordshire, and Gwynedd in North Wales. The fellowship and enjoyment of cycling continues undiminished: in Sunday runs into the countryside, long-distance touring, racing on road and track (especially at the Manchester Velodrome), and time-trialling. Political activity has been notable by its absence, and, sadly, many old-timers whose membership stretched back into the 1930s and 40s have gone. At the same time, however, individual members have been active in the movements against war, racism, and capitalist globalization. As in many other spheres, the early part of this century for the Clarion seems to be a period of increasing uncertainty, but there are still those of us who believe as strongly as ever that Socialism is the hope of the world in the years ahead.

Denis Pye
Bolton, Lancashire
October 2003

CONTENTS

Preface   page v

I   Cycling and Socialism   page 1
II   Robert Blatchford and The *Clarion*   page 4
III   'Advance Birmingham': Tom Groom   page 9
       and the First Clarion Cycling Club
IV   Easter Meets and the National Clarion   page 14
V   Propagating the Principles of Socialism   page 27
VI   Women, Cycling and the Clarion Vans   page 34
VII   Clarion Camps and Clubhouses   page 42
VIII   The Clarion Movement 1894-1914:   page 48
       A New Way of Life
IX   Blatchford, War and the Paper's Decline   page 54
X   Choirs, Vans and Clubhouses Between the Wars   page 59
XI   The National Clarion and Cycle Racing   page 62
XII   Peace Through Sport: The Clarion CC   page 66
       Against War and Fascism
XII   After Tom Groom: The National Clarion's   page 76
       Second Half-Century
XIV   Epilogue: The End of History?   page 85

       Bibliography and References   page 87

       Appendix I: National Clarion Cycling Club
       Easter Meets   page 88

       Appendix II: Clarion Cycling Club
       National Secretaries   page 89

       Index   page 89

Dedicated to

Wendy, John, Jennie, Mark and Sam,
And All Clarion Socialists

'Life may change, but it may fly not;
Hope can vanish, but can die not;
Truth be veiled, but still it burneth;
Love repulsed, but it returneth.'
P.B.Shelley
(set to music in the *Clarion Song Book*, 1906)

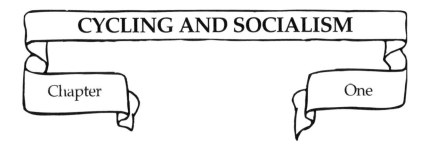

CYCLING AND SOCIALISM

Chapter   One

I n the early 1890s the bicycle was 'King of the Road'. Petrol-driven cars and lorries were rarely seen, and though horse-drawn vehicles – carts, cabs and carriages – still dominated the streets and roads, the bicycle was rapidly becoming the main means of personal transport for all but the poor, the old, the disabled and babes-in-arms. Here at last was a comparatively cheap form of travel to supplement the network of railways which by now stretched into every corner of the land.

The Safety Bicycle

The bicycle boom of the nineties had been stimulated by the introduction in the previous decade of what was called the 'Safety' to distinguish it from the inherently unsafe 'Ordinary' (sometimes called the high-wheeler or 'penny-farthing') which preceded it. By the late 1880s the pedal cycle had more or less taken the form with which we are familiar today: tubular-steel frame; pedals, cranks and chain; leather saddle; and equal-sized wheels with inflatable rubber tyres. As the obvious advantages of the Safety became better known, demand increased and hundreds of manufacturers established themselves throughout the  country in industrial areas. Improved production methods and competition steadily brought down prices, putting the bicycle within financial reach of the less well-off, though not the poorest.

In the early 1890s wages could be as little as a pound a week, or less, for those fortunate enough to be in work, but a second-hand machine might be found for not much more than two pounds. A new machine was expensive at ten pounds or more, even though you could pay by instalments. Yet it was increasingly apparent to the many writers of cycling columns in newspapers that prices were coming down year by year. When the Ordinary had reigned supreme in in the early 1880s cycling clubs were made up of comfortably-off gentlemen, but ten years later it seemed to many observers that a social revolution was under way as the bicycle craze spread first to lower middle-class men and women (like office-workers and shop assistants) and then to skilled manual workers.

Socialist Revival

At the same time as the Safety bicycle was being introduced there was a revival of the Socialist ideas which had seemed to fade in their appeal after the end of the Chartist movement in the 1850s. This reawakening was reflected in the formation of a number of Socialist organisations in the 1880s.

Between 1883 and 1884 the Democratic Federation, led by H.M.Hyndman, adopted a Socialist programme which included common ownership of the land, banks and railways, and an eight-hour day for workers. Re-named Social Democratic Federation (SDF) it suffered a breakaway when a group which included artist and writer William Morris left to form the short-lived Socialist League. By 1884 working-class men had achieved the right to vote in parliamentary elections and a few candidates supported by trade-unions were elected to 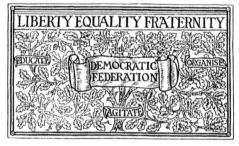 the House of Commons as 'Lib-Lab' (Liberal-Labour) MPs. Among them was Keir Hardie who realised, as did many other Socialists, that representation independent of the Liberal Party was needed. In Lancashire and Yorkshire industrial towns Independent Labour Parties were founded, and by 1893 the ILP was a national organisation.

The SDF and ILP were dedicated to the preaching of Socialism, and this was literally the practice in many places after 1891 when Labour Churches were set up by nonconformist ministers and their congregations, often using chapel buildings. The message was that the social evils of capitalism – poverty, ignorance and oppression – could only be overcome when the inequalities of competitive greed were replaced by the Co-operative Commonwealth. The aims and objects of the SDF were set out briefly:

Educate: We shall need all our intelligence.
Agitate: We shall need all our enthusiasm.
Organise: We shall need all our force.

The Fellowship of the Wheel

It seems in hindsight inevitable, given cycling's spectacular increase in popularity during the 1890s, that the men and women who answered the Socialist call would be enthusiasts for the pastime. The use of the bicycle seemed admirably suited to the beliefs of people dedicated to the spreading of what was to them a new religion of freedom and equality. Cycling was a means of transport available to nearly everybody, young or old, man or woman, whether in manual or white-collar work. It offered to members of a cycling club the health and freedom of the open road in company with others of like-mind.

Looking back from a vantage-point just before the first world war, Tom Tyas, Secretary of the Handforth Clarion Cyclists' Clubhouse, noted in an information brochure this "synchronisation" of the coming of the Safety bicycle with the spread of Socialism. He called it "a happy combination of natural forces". The bicycle, he wrote, "brought within easy reach all the things which the new philosophy taught [people] to enjoy". It offered an "escape from city life after the daily round of toil" and gave them "the power to roam on the King's Highway".

A luxury [he went on] hitherto almost the exclusive privilege of the rich was now within easy reach of all. The beauties of the countryside could be enjoyed by mere possession of the magic wheel ... Hence, Socialist Cycling Clubs, the product of fellowship and mutual help, sprang into existence all over the country.

Tom Tyas could have added that these clubs owed their existence to Robert Blatchford and his friends, who started the *Clarion* weekly paper in 1891.

ROBERT BLATCHFORD AND THE *CLARION*

Chapter   Two

Had there been no Robert Blatchford, there would have been no *Clarion*. Had there been no *Clarion*, there would have been no Clarion Cycling Club," wrote Tom Groom in his 1944 *Jubilee Souvenir*. "The older hands," he continued, "who have been through the early struggles, must be permitted to give their thanks and their gratitude to those who first fired their enthusiasm in the cause of Socialism. And the man they will always best remember is Robert Blatchford."

Early Years and Army Life

Robert Peel Glanville Blatchford was born at Maidstone in 1851, the second child of a couple who made a precarious living from playing small parts in dramatic productions as they moved about the country. His father died when Robert was only two years old, leaving his mother, his older brother Montague and himself to endure desperate poverty as they travelled from town to town, often on foot. Eventually they settled in Halifax where Mrs Blatchford earned eight shillings a week as a dressmaker. While his brother was apprenticed to a lithographic printer, Robert was taken on by a firm of brushmakers.

Five minutes late to work one morning, he found himself locked out, as was the disciplinary practice in those days. Leaving the job, his family and Halifax behind, he took to the road. He begged a free passage to Yarmouth on a small coastal vessel and then walked to London. Here, after failing to find work, he was forced to carry on sleeping rough. At last, in 1871, he was driven by hunger and the cold to enlist in the army at Tower Gates. The 'Queen's shilling' which he received for signing on, he gave to a girl he had sheltered with the previous night under Waterloo Bridge.

Blatchford served in the army for six years; his physical health improved and he benefited from some basic education. More importantly, he found a comradeship which he never forgot, and gained in confidence and self-esteem. Having reached the rank of sergeant he took his discharge and found a job as timekeeper and storeman with the Weaver Navigation Company in Northwich, Cheshire, at a guinea a week. In 1880 when his wage was raised to thirty shillings he married Sarah Crossley (Sally) whom he had first met at the brush works in Halifax.

Writer and Journalist

In his spare time Robert began to write short stories and in 1882 succeeded in getting one published (title: "The Militiaman") in a paper called *The Yorkshireman*. For this he was paid half-a-guinea, which encouraged him to go on writing. By 1884 he was contributing a humorous weekly column of four thousand words (still written in his spare time) to a Leeds paper for a guinea a time. Not long after, an old army friend introduced him to a young Manchester journalist, A.M.Thompson, who recommended him for a full-time job on a London paper, *Bell's Life*. This brought in what was then a good income of four pounds a week. He adopted the pen-name 'Nunquam Dormio' (literally, 'I Never Sleep') which was the slogan printed under the paper's masthead. And it was in the *Bell's Life* office that he first met Edward Fay, a six-foot two, eighteen-stone humorous writer – pen-name 'The Bounder'.

1887 was a disastrous year for the Blatchfords. Two of their three children died, and *Bell's Life* closed down. Robert, with Sarah and young Winifred, went back north to Manchester to start work on one of Edward Hulton's papers, the *Sunday Chronicle*, in Withy Grove. His friend A.M.Thompson was still there, and Edward Fay became the paper's London correspondent. It was with the *Sunday Chronicle* that Blatchford made his reputation and gained a large readership as 'Nunquam', writing passionately each week about the appalling living conditions endured by poor people in Manchester.

Socialist Conversion

Later in life Blatchford remembered that the bulk of working-class dwellings in Manchester were slums at this time: "Sixty thousand houses and not a single decent habitation." He visited the courts, alleys and streets with William Palmer, an illustrator on the *Chronicle*'s staff, who took photographs and sketched what they found. Another newspaper accused them of "thrusting the filth of the slums under the noses of decent people." Blatchford believed that the effect on readers was negligible: the effect on them was more lasting.

Joe Waddington, a reader of Nunquam's articles who was an unemployed joiner and a Socialist activist, suggested that he should go inside the houses and cellars to meet the people living in them. "I set off alone," wrote Blatchford forty years later, "and went hopefully into a small court in a penurious district of Hulme". The memory of what he found there and in Ancoats remained vivid, painful and grim. He remembered that he paid for a doctor to visit a baby whose father was unemployed. It was too late; the child died soon after of bronchitis. Blatchford used his influence to find a job on the railway for another man; he would have to walk four miles and start work at 4 am for a pittance.

Nunquam's bitter exposures of life in the slums grew ever more impassioned. But however popular it was with readers, the paper's owner and its editor were not pleased with this kind of journalism. Matters came to a head when Blatchford declared in print his allegiance to Socialism – the only way to a better future. It seems that he was finally convinced after reading a pamphlet, "What Is Socialism?" written by William Morris and H.M.Hyndman.

The inevitable row with Edward Hulton soon followed and Nunquam walked out after telling him, "You will not have Socialism in your paper – and I won't write anything else." He recalled many years later that in March 1891 he had a fat bank balance and a salary of £1,000 a year (perhaps the equivalent of about £40,000 today) and by October he was out of work and heavily in debt.

'The Perisher'

Alex Thompson, Edward Fay, William Palmer and another sympathiser, Robert Suthers, all resigned from the *Chronicle* with Robert Blatchford. They were joined by Robert's brother Montague who also gave up his job, and on the 12th December 1891 they "went to sea in a sieve" by bringing out the first issue of a penny Socialist weekly, *The Clarion* (fondly referred to as the 'Perisher') from a tiny office in Corporation Street, Manchester. There were printing difficulties caused by cheap paper, and the publicity posters were washed away by heavy rain, but 40,000 copies were sold, largely on the strength of Nunquam's already-established popularity with working-class readers of the *Sunday Chronicle*.

In his first leading article Blatchford wrote:

> *The Clarion* is a paper meant by its owners and writers to tell the truth as they see it, frankly and without fear. *The Clarion* may not always be right, but it will always be sincere. Its staff do not claim

ᗒhe ᗒLARIOᑎ
EᗪITEᗪ · Bᵞ · ᑎUᑎQUAᗰ

to be witty or wise, but they do claim to be honest. They write not for factions; but for the people. They fight not for victory; but for the truth. They do not seek to dazzle, but to please; not to anger, but to convince. Wheresoever wrong exists they will try to expose it. Towards baseness, cowardice, self-seeking or roguery, no matter where or in what class it may appear, they will show no mercy ...

The essence of this new journalism, for it is a new journalism, and a journalism created by the men now risking this venture, is variety. I would, therefore, beg our serious friends to remember that truth may lie under a smile as well as under a frown, and to our merry friends would say that a jest is none the less hilarious when it comes from the heart. The policy of *The Clarion* is a policy of humanity, a policy not of party, sect or creed; but of justice, reason and mercy.

It has been said that Blatchford's Socialism was based on ethics, not economics. His gift was to be able to write movingly about injustice and inequality and to present a Socialist argument clearly. His founder-colleagues ('The Board', as they became known) laid down no agreed policy or programme, so that the paper became an open forum for different Socialist groups and individuals.

After the editorial office moved to Fleet Street, London, in 1895 circulation grew steadily to reach over 80,000 by 1908. *The Clarion* sold well not only because it was written plainly and unpretentiously, but because it was entertaining, and professionally produced. Apart from political articles and editorials which aimed to "make Socialists", as Blatchford put it, by explaining the principles of Socialism "in the simplest and best language at our command", there was much which merely aimed to amuse. There were regular weekly features on music, theatre, books and sport (including cycling), plus a *Children's Corner* and a *Woman's Letter*.

Nunquam, The Bounder, Dangle (A.M. Thompson), Mont Blong (Montague Blatchford), Whiffly Puncto (William Palmer) and the rest were not only admired but loved by readers. In tens of thousands of working-class homes the members of the Clarion Board were friends rather than just names. When, in the summer of 1894, a group of Birmingham readers heard rumours of financial difficulties they wrote in:

> Its going down means personally an interest in life gone; socially a serious blow to our movement... Although none of the undersigned has ever met the *Clarion* staff personally our sense of comradeship towards you is as vivid as though we met each day ... The *Clarion* is too good to lose.

One advertisement for the paper declared: "There is nothing like it. There never was anything like it. There never will be anything like it." And the reason why this was no empty slogan is that the *Clarion*, unlike other Socialist papers, espoused a Socialism which was not in

"CLARION JOE."

the least solemn, difficult, highbrow, dreary, theoretical or dogmatic, but rather a way of life to be enjoyed here and now, in which men and women, young and old, would live in fellowship with each other in their everyday work and leisure activities.

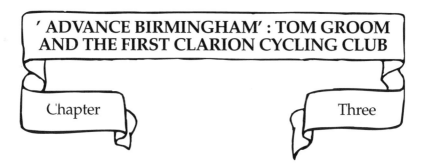

' ADVANCE BIRMINGHAM' : TOM GROOM AND THE FIRST CLARION CYCLING CLUB

Chapter   Three

Without the Clarion Cycling Clubs the circulation and influence of the *Clarion* would not have reached the heights which they eventually achieved. It is said that in the twenty years before the First World War a Clarion cyclist, almost by definition, was someone riding a machine with saddlebag crammed or carrier piled high with copies of the paper, all of which would eventually be sold or given away.

The First Meetings

It all started one Monday night in February at the Labour Church on Constitution Hill in Birmingham where the young Tom Groom, at that time Secretary of the Church, had called a meeting to discuss how best the members could "combine the pleasures of cycling with the propaganda of Socialism". Five other men turned up, and the minutes of the meeting were recorded as follows:

Meeting held at Bond Street Labour Church,
Monday February 26th, 1894.
Present: Messrs. Atkinson, Powell, Richards,
Muir, Groom and Thompson.
Mr. Groom voted to the Chair.
The following rules were accepted:
(1) that the Club be called the Socialists' Cycling Club
(2) that the subscription be 2s.6d. per season, payable in advance
(3) that the Club be managed by a Committee composed of the Captain, Vice-Captain, Secretary, and four members, the officers being members of the Bond Street Labour Church
(4) Any vacancy on the committee shall be filled up at the next meeting.

There was already a vacancy: Harry Atkinson was elected Captain,

W. Powell Vice-Captain, and Chris Thompson Secretary-Treasurer, but there were only three others to be Committee members: Tom Groom, Steve Muir and J. Cruwys Richards. At a second meeting on Wednesday 7th March the additional member turned up – Walter White – and they voted unanimously to rescind Rule 1 and change their name to the Clarion Cycling Club, after their favourite weekly paper. They went on to arrange an Easter Tour and to accept Chris Thompson's design for a badge – a Clarion 'instrument' (a trumpet) supporting the letters of the paper's title. Within a month they had decided to order two dozen of the badges in hallmarked silver. (They were soon to be sold nationally at 1/8d each – about 9p – postage included.) At the same meeting they agreed to invite the Bounder – E.F. Fay – to be their President, and to start a photograph album. Looking back twenty-one years later Tom Groom wrote:

> The *Clarion* had made Socialists of us; it was the *Clarion* which had brought us together; it was the *Clarion* which had inspired the Socialist Movement with that spirit of cheerfulness and fellowship which was so badly needed; and it was the *Clarion* that had given us the Bounder and his gorgeous contempt for respectability.

Tom had been a committed Socialist since joining the SDF in 1886 at the age of fifteen, and a cyclist since 1888 when he acquired his first machine, an Old Ordinary. He was in no doubt that the paper played an essential role in combining enthusiasm for cycling with missionary Socialist zeal. Indeed, it was he more than anyone else who was instrumental in bringing this about for thousands of people.

Easter Tour 1894

In the issue of the *Clarion* dated Saturday 28th April 1894 there appeared an article with the headline "Advance Birmingham!" and sub-headed, "Being an Account of the Clarion Cycle Club Easter Tour". It was contributed by 'The O'Groomie O' who described how seven cyclists, "cold, hungry and half-awake," set out from Birmingham "on a dirty, dark, damp, dismal, dreary morning at 7-15 am". They loaded their bikes on to the train at Snow Hill station for the short trip to Wolverhampton, where they ate some breakfast. As they left the town, the sun came out and the birds began to sing. Their spirits lifted, they pedalled on to Bridgnorth, there, as the writer put it, to 'Bounderise' ("verb irregular – very – meaning: to imbibe liquors of various degrees of strength, to assimilate resuscitating comestibles, to walk on one's heels, and to generally spread one's self.") On they went, through Arley to Bewdley for an overnight bed-and-breakfast stay. Next day's route (it was Easter Saturday) took them through Stourport, Ombursley and Pershore to Worcester. They rode in single file through the city.

Suddenly, the first man rang his bell and dismounted, the others following suit. The first man spake not, but pointed with trembling delight to where they sold the *Clarion* ... We all marched in, in order, purchased our *Clarions* and then, as solemnly, walked out, mounted our machines and proceeded on our way as men who had had glimpses of higher things.

At Evesham they 'Bounderised' again. "Good Lord! How we did eat! For half-an-hour we raised not our eyes and spake not a word, but steadily thought on the Bounder."

By the evening of Easter Sunday they were back in Birmingham in time for the service at Bond Street Labour Church. Tom Groom's report summed up the tour: "We had spent as grand a holiday as possible. Ah-h-h! It was glorious! Say no man lives until he has been on tour with the Clarion CC. Till then he but exists."

First Season

The Easter Tour was not the only one that year. At Whitsun they went south, finishing in London where they took the train home. In August they went to North Wales (this became an annual holiday tour), visiting Beddgelert, Criccieth, Betws-y-Coed, Dolgellau and Barmouth.

A fixture-card was printed with destinations for regular runs on Wednesday evenings, Saturday afternoons and Sundays. The first Saturday each month was set aside for cyclists to meet non-cycling members at some beauty-spot in the countryside to have a picnic meal and play games on the grass. On some summer Saturdays groups of children from the slums of Birmingham were taken on outings and fed out of the proceeds of the 'Cinderella Club' fund-raising promoted by Nunquam in the *Clarion*.

Although the founding members of Birmingham Clarion CC were all men, they soon began to recruit women into membership – the first in July 1894. This was something of a novelty at that time, for the early cycling clubs of the 1880s had usually restricted admission to 'gentlemen'.

Meanwhile, developments in Birmingham had not gone unnoticed in other parts of the country. Tom Groom's reports in the *Clarion* sparked the enthusiasm of cyclist readers elsewhere, and by the end of 1894 four more Clarion CCs had been formed: in the Potteries (at Hanley), and in Liverpool, Bradford and Barnsley. From the beginning the Clubs were in contact with each other. An inter-club meet between Birmingham and Hanley took place at Rugeley in July and at Lichfield in August. The two Clubs met up with each other on tour in North Wales that summer. And when Birmingham arranged a Clarion CC Supper in October, Potteries members were invited. Sixty people turned up for this event, which was presided over by the Bounder himself. As Frank Leeming ('Swiftsure'), the *Clarion*'s first regular cycling columnist declared: "All cyclists should join one of the Clarion CCs, if it is not only to cultivate the acquaintance of our Birmingham comrades." "They were," he enthused, "full of good fellowship and humanity," and, "worth a guinea a box!" Tom Groom hit the mark in his report of the Welsh tour, which turned out to be shorter than originally planned: "This club ain't great at distances. What this club wants is not a speedometer but a boozometer."

In September 1894 'The O'Groomie-O' sent an end-of-season report to the paper:

Our first season has been a great success all round. We started early in March with five members and now number thirty. We have had very good average attendances on the runs, and those runs have been glorious – not a dull one on the fixture-card; each with its own pleasant memories, and the whole crowded with the sense of good fellowship. The spirit of comradeship has increased with every run. And how can a fellow help but be chummy after a good run along Warwickshire roads and lanes; a splendid feed at the journey's end (and, shades of the Bounder, how we have learned to eat!) and a quiet run home in the dark ... Our Socials have given great joy. The first Saturday's run in each month is arranged to some place where the non-cyclists can meet us and help make things hum. The last of these for this year was held on the first last at Lichfield. The Potteries Clarionettes arrived and great was the joy thereof. The weather was fine, the roads were good and the going rattling. The tea at the Dolphin was splendid and the smoker (concert) which followed one of the most successful among a crowd of successes ... The Potteries CCC started homewards just after 10 pm – 32 miles and pitch dark. We haven't heard of them since ... On the whole we are very satisfied with our season. We have made real friends among ourselves; we have fraternised with Hanley, scattered *Clarions* and leaflets, helped the Red Van [a horse-drawn publicity caravan used by the Land Restoration League – author], helped at the Cinderella outings, and have the Bounder for President. What club can hope for more? Next year we hope to fraternise with other Clarion CCs which exist. Why not a big meet early in the spring – say Easter – of all the Clarion cyclists?

EASTER MEETS AND THE NATIONAL CLARION

Chapter Four

Support for the idea of a big Easter Meet of all Clarion cyclists was soon in evidence. Bradford CCC's *Clarion* correspondent 'Peddlar' wrote in to announce: "We shall be pleased to fall in at the meat (sic) ... Why should not some hundred Clarion cyclists spend a few days together if some suitable centre could only be spotted out? We should hope to bring a little crowd with us from this end. With our President, Ben Tillett, riding at our head, we should be bound to arrive."

In the summer of 1894 the members of Birmingham Clarion CC had arranged a picnic at Ashbourne in Derbyshire, with an overnight stay at the George and Dragon. Swiftsure, in the *Clarion*'s *Cycling Notes*, then suggested that there should be a camp there the following year, with "sports and excursions". At the end of December Tom Groom reported that he was already trying to arrange the promised Easter Meet at Ashbourne. And in a letter which appeared in the same issue of the paper, a correspondent C.D. Reekie announced his intention of joining the soon-to-be-formed Manchester Clarion Cycling Club. (An ILP Wheelers Club had been going in the city since April 1894.) "Like all Socialists," he wrote, "I am a dreamer and have dreamt of that great day when the gigantic ILP picnic is to be held, and I fancied I saw a team race between the different Klarion Klubs for the Klarion Kup."

Ashbourne 1895

By March 1895 anxious enquiries were being made about the Easter Meet by newly-formed Clarion CCs, including those at Nottingham, Newcastle, Leeds, Rochdale, Blackburn, Burnley, Wigan, Hyde and Nelson. F.G. Browne, the new Birmingham Secretary, asked them to send him an estimate of the numbers of those intending to be there, advising that all clubs should aim to send at least one or two delegates. He was already sketching out a programme for the weekend. The Meet would, he hoped, be "a means of further cementing those bonds which should unite the rapidly increasing band of Clarion Cyclists." There would be an inter-club run on the Saturday, returning for tea at 5pm, with a "smoking concert" to end the day. On the morning of Easter Sunday they would all walk to Dove Dale for lunch. Here, a Conference at 1pm would consider resolutions to form a National Clarion Cycling Club, adopt a badge and a uniform code of rules for all the clubs. It was confidently suggested that the *Clarion*'s 'Board' would be there. "England expects every Clarion cyclist to be present," the Birmingham secretary concluded. Swiftsure's promise that all would be welcome, whether cyclists or not, was somewhat rash since it was known that only about eighty people could be guaranteed suitably-priced accommodation in Ashbourne.

Good Friday came and the hundred or so who were riding to the Meet set out: half-a-dozen from Yorkshire, about fifty from Birmingham, Nottingham and the Potteries, ten from Liverpool, and over forty from the Manchester area. Some cyclists came from places with no Clarion CC yet, like Sheffield and Halifax. All these, together with the many non-cyclists who travelled by train, made up a total claimed at first to be nearly 200, though later it was agreed that a more realistic figure would be 120. True to their promise, members of the *Clarion* paper's staff arrived – including Nunquam (the 'Chief') with the Bounder and Dangle. Mont Blong and Whiffly Puncto took the train to Derby, then cycled to Ashbourne, calling at two pubs on the way. Whiffly came off on a hill and tore his "six-and-sixpenny knickerbocker trousers!" Eventually they were welcomed into Ashbourne by a group of young men standing on the bridge who shouted, "Boots!"; to which they gave the Clarion reply, "Spurs!" (By this date, all *Clarion* readers were familiar with Blatchford's "soldier stories" in which men spinning yarns in the barrack-room after lights-out tested the attentiveness of their audience by interjecting the word "Boots!" at intervals, expecting a chorus of "Spurs!" in reply.)

Friday night's 'smoker', or concert, in the George and Dragon, the Meet Headquarters, was an impromptu entertainment of songs and recitations – "a right merry evening of good fellowship". A Liverpool comrade sang the 'Red Flag'. 'Daisy Bell' (about the couple on a "bicycle made for two") was sung in chorus, with a zither accompaniment; and the 'Lone Scout' (Bob Manson, a well-known Liverpool activist) presented the Bounder with a trophy – the top from a street-lamp!

Next day's cycle ride to Alton Towers in the bracing Derbyshire air freshened up those who took part, in time for another 'smoker' that night. Little wonder that Dangle suggested afterwards it should have been called the Ashbourne Meet and Drink!

Mont Blong described the events of Easter Sunday, 14th April 1895, in the following week's *Clarion*:

> ... we marched two-hundred strong to Dove Dale. Preceded by the (Potteries) Clarion bugler, the Clarion Scouts took the open road in fine style and as they passed the market-place raised a Clarion whoop, which so alarmed the Yeomanry who were preparing for a church-parade, that one or two dropped off their perches.
> It was a faultless morning with a wide sweep of pale blue sky, without the suspicion of a cloud, and a great strong English breeze which invigorated everybody.

The first Annual Conference of Clarion Cycling Clubs started at about 1pm on the lawn just outside the Izaak Walton Hotel in Dovedale. Dangle was in the chair, "which office he carried out, to the satisfaction of everyone, lying down on the flat of his front elevation". To start off, Tom Groom gave a short account of Birmingham Clarion CC's first year and then went on to talk about national organisation. It was, he thought, Leonard Hall of Manchester ILP who first suggested a National Clarion Cycling Club during a visit to Birmingham. Tom then went on to discuss what was to be a perennial source of controversy within the Club in the years to come. "I should not like the (rule) adopted ... that none but Socialists or ILP or SDF be admitted as members," he said. That would be absurd. Anyone who cared to join should be admitted, only reserving the management of the Club to those connected with some distinctly Socialist body. "By giving the non-Socialist who may join us Clarion reasoning and Clarion comradeship we may soon turn him into a bona fide Socialist ... let us be easy in our pleasures."

The Clarion Cycling Club's mission, in his view, was to spread good fellowship. The cyclist was particularly fitted for this. "Little troubles keep him sympathetic – punctures, chains that break, nuts that loosen, lamps that won't burn, etc. Runs in the country and glorious sights prevent him becoming narrow and bigoted. The mere exercise of cycling is the best antidote to a sluggish liver yet devised."

> We are not neglectful of our Socialism [he went on]; the frequent contrasts a cyclist gets between the beauties of nature and the dirty squalor of towns make him more anxious than ever to abolish the present system. To get healthy exercise is not necessarily to be selfish. To attend to the social side of our work is not necessarily to neglect the more serious part. To spread good fellowship is ... the most important work of Clarion Cycling Clubs. Then, perhaps, the 'One Socialist Party' would be more possible and we should get

less of those squabbles among Socialists which make me doubt whether they understand even the first part of their name.

Finally, Tom reiterated the words of William Morris in *A Dream of John Ball* which were to be used so often by Clarion people: "Fellowship is heaven, and lack of fellowship is hell: fellowship is life and lack of fellowship is death."

The business part of the conference was commendably brief. It was unanimously resolved that a National Clarion Cycling Club be formed; that a sub-committee consisting of Atkinson (Birmingham), Ranstead (Liverpool), and Sutcliffe (Manchester) be formed to draw up rules for the CCC; that the Birmingham badge be adopted as a national badge; and that an annual meeting of clubs be held. The conference came to an abrupt conclusion. As the printed report put it: "Dangle discovering that the grass was a trifle damp, the meeting was broken up."

The high point of this first Easter Meet seems to have been an open-air Socialist meeting in the market-place. According to Mont Blong, "It stirred Ashbourne to its very foundations. And, sooth to say, it wanted stirring badly." One speaker, Jimmy Sexton from Liverpool, was heckled by a pompous farm bailiff from the Duke of Devonshire's Chatsworth estate who repeatedly shouted, "Liar! Liar!" He was invited to explain, but could only bluster: "We don't want any of that sort of talk here." Having declined to take the rostrum himself and refusing to answer any questions about his views, he went off. Another heckler was later referred to as the "Beery-person." He was a Tory, "a conspicuous light and adornment to the Duke of Devonshire's tenantry". He staggered in and out of the 'Dragon' declaring loudly, "Aw don't know owt, and aw don't want to know owt." An account of the meeting in the *Ashbourne News* ended: "... things were pretty lively, the Socialists winding up with three cheers for their faith and their hearers replying with God Save the Queen".

News of the Meet even reached Fleet Street. On April 16th the *London Evening News* reported briefly:

Many quiet nooks in the Midlands and North of England have been invaded during the last few days by a band of cycling socialists who describe themselves as the 'Clarion Club.' They have been endeavouring, with scant measure of success, to propagate their views in the country districts and to advertise the socialist organ after which their club is named.

The sub-committee of three elected at Ashbourne duly met in Birmingham ten days later and formulated a short set of rules for the new-born

National Clarion CC. The object was to be "the association of the various Clarion Cycling Clubs for the purpose of Socialist propaganda and for promoting inter-club runs between the clubs of different towns". Rules were suggested for local clubs, among them one which stipulated that the officers should be members of "a recognised Socialist organisation" Another empowered the local committee to devote any surplus cash to the Labour Movement. Standard whistle calls for club runs were suggested: "one blow: single file; two blows: steady; three blows: dismount".

Bakewell 1896

It was the end of the year before the next annual meet venue began to be discussed in the cycling columns of the *Clarion*. Manchester CCC, by now the biggest of the local clubs, supported Bakewell. (Derbyshire was seen as the most central area for ease of access since most of the rapidly increasing number of Clarion CCs were to be found in the industrial towns of the Midlands and North of England.) Others suggested a postal vote on both the place and date. Nottingham members put forward the claims of their own city as a suitable venue, arguing that it would be appropriate because the ILP annual conference was to be held there at Easter 1896. Swiftsure argued against this, revealing that he shared the view of a sizeable minority of members which was to remain stubbornly present over the years. He was an ILP member, but did not want the National Clarion to be turned into another "semi-political organisation". "We might as well," he wrote, "form Clarion cricket, football and golf clubs and endeavour to make those mediums for militant socialist propaganda." Another suggestion (from the minority of Clubs located in the South of England) was that instead of an Easter Meet there should be two annual meets at Whitsun – one in Oxford and one in the North.

By February 1896 the National Committee (as the three-man sub-committee now styled itself) was reporting that they were "practically decided" on Bakewell at Easter. They asked local Clubs to send in items for the Conference. Manchester submitted resolutions asking for a national members' "guide-book and directory of accommodation", and for the organisation of national racing events with prizes.

Recommended routes to Bakewell were included in the *Clarion*'s Cycling Notes. Those coming from the north were warned that they would encounter some hilly cycling. Brakes would be a necessity for "all but the most expert back-pedallers", while coasting with feet off the pedals was not advised.

Arrangements for the Meet were completed by the end of March.

Headquarters would be at the Royal Oak where a hundred could dine at one sitting and there would be stabling for all machines. On arrival, members and friends would be asked to enter their names in the book and McAtkinson (Harry Atkinson of Birmingham) would supply addresses for lodgings. Accommodation for a hundred had been secured.

Saturday's cycle runs would take in Haddon Hall and Chatsworth House, and that evening's smoking concert would be under the direction of 'Auld Reekie' (Charlie Reekie of Manchester) and the O'Groomio. The Conference would take place at lunch-time on the Sunday, outdoors again, in Monsal Dale where bread, cheese, ginger beer and "nut-brown ale" would be available.

Many more Clarionettes crowded into Bakewell than had been expected. Atkinson had to find accommodation for over 300 out of the 350 or so who signed the 'muster-roll'. Swiftsure commented in the paper: "I question whether anything like it has ever occurred before in this country." The attendance simply reflected the spectacular growth of the National Clarion, from about thirty local clubs early in 1896 to over sixty by the end of the year.

Mont Blong wrote a colourful description of the scene when he arrived at the Meet accompanied by Whiffly Puncto and their bicycles:

> We found Bakewell had been taken possession of by the Clarion cyclists, some two hundred of whom were gathered together in the large hall of the Royal Oak, apparently enjoying themselves, and trying to look as though sitting was quite conducive. But one hardly ever knows. There we found Nunquam wearing a blue cap and a moderate smile; Dangle enveloped in a cloud of tobacco smoke and gloom, his quaintly-carved beard surmounted by a brown sombrero of generous dimensions; and the Candid Friend [William Ranstead from Tilston in Cheshire] in complete bicycle rig of the most convincing nature; and they were surrounded by a cheerful crowd of bikers of all sorts and sizes who had come in – and were still coming in – from all points of the compass.

Tom Groom recalled that half-a-dozen members rode all the way from Bristol, arriving at two in the morning. One came on an Ordinary and Tom joked: "He had to have a morphine injection before he could get his legs to stop pushing around the pedals of his machine."

Mont Blong was in the chair ("a cane one") for the National Clarion's second Annual Conference on Easter Sunday at Monsal Dale. Everybody else sat on the grass or on walls. Of the actual proceedings, little can be said, except that it lasted less than an hour and nothing came of it. The three-man National Committee had held only one meeting during the preceding year, at which (as they reported) nothing was done. Their report was so unsatisfactory, Mont Blong recalled later, that they were all re-elected for another twelve months, with the addition to their number of Tom Groom.

Though some were critical of such an unbusinesslike approach to a conference, Robert Blatchford was well-satisfied. He thought that the National Clarion CC's example "might with advantage be followed by some of the more pretentious factions of the same name that have been held lately". (He probably meant the ILP Conference.) "It was," he wrote, "a model because nothing was done that caused pain or discomfort to anyone, or to bind anyone to a hard and fast line. There was no officialism, no wire-pulling, and no attempt to interfere in any way with the perfect freedom and local independence of any club connected with the union."

The inhabitants of Bakewell and surrounding areas were also happy with the weekend's events despite the fears of local dignitaries, especially the clergy, about the prospect of Socialists meeting in their town. The landlord of the Royal Oak and the reporter from the *Derbyshire Times* were impressed with the behaviour and good humour of the people now widely known as Clarionettes. Perhaps this satisfaction was related to the fact that there had been no outdoor propaganda meeting, or any other attempt to preach Socialism – an omission which upset the activists. Yet for Mont Blong the fact that those attending the Meet were "good-tempered, full of fun and frolic, and considerate did more to dispel prejudice and popularise Socialism than the most earnest oratory could have accomplished".

Leek 1897

In view of the rapid rate at which Clarion CCs were being formed (more than seventy were in existence by the beginning of 1897) it was thought by many members that a much bigger town would be needed to accommodate the 500 or more expected at the next Easter Meet. Chester and Shrewsbury were suggested. In March 1897 a postal vote took place in which Chester had the support of nine clubs, but, surprisingly, Leek in Staffordshire had the support of twelve clubs. (The majority did not send in a vote.) The attraction of Leek seems to have been the William Morris Labour Church, newly opened in a former Friends' Meeting House. A 200-year-old building, it was surrounded by trees and contained work by Socialist artist Walter Crane, and by Morris himself. The Meet Headquarters, however, were to be at the Swan Hotel, which had a concert room to hold 400. The programme was planned to follow the pattern established by the two earlier Annual Meets, with the additions of a Cinderella conference on Saturday afternoon and a lantern slide lecture on Sunday night. Among the resolutions submitted for the Cycling Club's Annual Conference was one from Bristol which insisted that: "All CCC's should state on their cards of membership:- Object: To propagate the principles of Socialism." Bolton urged the adoption of a 'national cap'. Bob Manson (the Lone Scout) wrote to the *Clarion* from Liverpool to express his concern about the absence of specific plans for Socialist activity at the Meet, pointing out that, "If Clarion CCs exist with no other object than wearing pretty costumes and riding about the country to festive gatherings then there is little justification for their being, and none for their name."

As it turned out, the main concern of the 1897 Leek Easter Meet seems to have been the weather. Tom Groom remembered it as "the leakiest Meet of them all", for it rained most of the time. The Conference, held outdoors again at Rudyard and attended by most of the 450 or so members at the Meet, escaped the rain, but there was such a strong wind that speakers could only be heard with difficulty. Seven resolutions were disposed of in thirty minutes and according to Tom Groom "leg-pulling rather than business was the order of the day". Some of those present condemned the lack of serious political discussion, but Tom still maintained that the main purpose of the Meet was "mutual pleasure". Although they were Socialists, making rules and regulations about propaganda work was inappropriate. Apathetic members, he believed, could only be shamed into activity. For him the growth of the National Clarion CC depended on freedom, autonomy and a loose organisation. This was why the National Committee had appeared to do nothing during the year and yet were re-elected. In any case, a meeting with a smaller number of delegates would, he thought, make decisions more effectively than a mass Conference.

Robert Blatchford, however, claimed to have seen at Leek "signs of northerners wanting to clog the wheels with red tape". In his view the Annual Conference should be more like a picnic, with long speeches, rulings and complicated resolutions tabooed: "No law, no officials, no constitutions, no cackle." He criticised the Lone Scout's enthusiasm for propaganda, which had been satisfied in the end with an open-air meeting in Leek market-place. Blatchford still believed that the most powerful Socialist influence at the Annual Meet should be the example and behaviour of Clarionettes – "a silent argument". He was, he wrote, "sick of platforms, harangues and politics".

The *Clarion*'s 'Post-Bag' of readers' letters was filled for weeks with the controversy. Correspondents sided either with Nunquam ("our principles are shown by our conduct") or with the Lone Scout ("respectable behaviour alone is not sufficient") Blatchford explained his position: that there was no need for an Annual Conference since a postal referendum of all members on important issues was more democratic. And open-air propaganda meetings, he believed, were nowhere near as influential as the paper. He objected to all discipline, regimentation or control. "No leaders, no rules, no delegates, no machinery!" he thundered in an editorial.

Chester 1898

Reports of the following year's Easter Meet give the impression that Blatchford's views had carried most weight. About 500 members signed the muster-roll and for the first time could buy an illustrated programme instead of the souvenir booklet produced after the previous gatherings. It included details of the (by now) customary evening concerts, but this timethere was to be a lantern slide lecture about "Ancient Chester" on the Sunday night rather than a Socialist rally. The Conference would take place on the bank of the River Dee as part of a Saturday afternoon "river picnic" following a trip by steamboats to Eaton Hall.

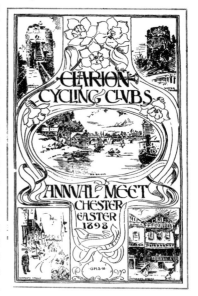

In the issue of the *Clarion* which came out on the weekend after the Meet, Nunquam noted with pleasure that the it had been "almost solely for pleasure," despite Bob Manson's plea for more political content. At the riverbank conference, after an hour's discussion about the composition of the National Committee, an un-named "quiet man" from Birmingham remarked in a casual way that as the National Committee had nothing at all to do, and couldn't do it if they had, it would perhaps be as well to abolish it all together. The chairman (Dangle again) who had fallen asleep on the grass was suddenly awakened at this point by a lighted cigarette in his ear and declared the suggestion carried. So the National Committee ceased to exist. "Some day," Blatchford commented, "the British public will do without the Houses of Parliament in the same way, and for the same reasons."

Two weeks later Tom Groom signed his report of the Meet: "The ex-Secretary of the ex-National Committee of the Very-Much-Alive NCCC." In later years, however, he remembered the Chester conference for the presence of two plain-clothes policemen who had been sent, in his words, to "nip sedition in the bud". They were fat, red-faced men who were highly amused by the proceedings they had been ordered to observe. Afterwards, one of them reported: "If these chaps kill anybody, it will be from laughing." It emerged that the Chester police had also over-reacted by calling up reserves to cope with the social disorder which might be caused by such a large gathering of Socialists in the city.

1899-1913

As the years passed, the programme for the Annual Meet followed the well-established pattern set by the gatherings staged in the early years – with only minor variations. There were concerts and dances on the Friday and Saturday nights, with Clarion choirs and bands, recitations (mostly humorous) and songs (mostly comic) by well-known and talented members. Conferences were held, not only for the Cycling Club but for other Clarion organisations as well. Mass cycle rides went off to local places of interest, and a huge group photograph was always taken, with prints widely sold afterwards. Sunday night was the usual time for lantern slide shows as well as an indoor Socialist public meeting. Despite the controversies of 1897, this kind of rally became the norm in addition to an afternoon meeting outdoors.

At Skipton in 1899 an attendance of over 400 proved too many for the lodgings (or 'billets') arranged. Bedding had to be quickly hired and fifty beds made up on the floor of the Temperance Hall. Even then, some were forced to seek shelter and warmth in the railway station waiting-room. It was at this Meet that the Conference (held outdoors again on the edge of Rombalds Moor) revived the three-man National Committee and the first real National Secretary was elected – though J.D. Sutcliffe from Manchester ('The Cheery One') and Tom Groom had both done this work previously. He was J. Taylor Clarke ('Jatece') who had a printing business in Stalybridge and produced attractively-illustrated Easter Meet programmes.

The following year, at Shrewsbury, conflict between the Clarionettes and soldiers of the Shropshire Light Infantry threatened, but the men from the barracks were quickly won over. Gales had deterred all but the strongest from riding to the meet and the attendance was lower than expected. This led to a financial loss which had to be covered by donations afterwards. The Conference, held round the bandstand in a park, lasted all of four minutes; just long enough to abolish the National Committee again – though it continued to meet, of course! A return to Bakewell in 1901 produced the first written Annual Conference Minutes when the meeting was held indoors for the first time. J. Taylor Clarke recorded that, "... about forty officers of the clubs met and discussed a number of resolutions. As a very large number of members were in the adjoining room, it was decided to hold the conference immediately after the concert instead of waiting till the Sunday morning". The resolutions were directed at bringing some order to the NCCC, principally one which resulted in the decision to raise a national levy of one penny per member at the end of each season, when membership was at its highest. In the National Committee of three which was elected one was to represent the South (T.Hore), one the Midlands (Tom Groom), and one the North ("JTC", the National Secretary.) There was also some discussion about the possibility of having three Meets each year, at Easter, Whitsun and August Bank Holiday, for the North, Midlands and South respectively. Regional meets had, in fact, been organised since 1896, so the well-established Southern Meet at Whitsun and the Scottish Meet at August Bank Holiday continued to be held as well as the national Easter event.

Outdoor conferences were not completely finished with. Unintentionally the one at the Stafford Meet in 1902 met in a doorway! When it was found that no-one had booked a separate hall big enough to hold all those who wanted to attend they went round to the Old Baptist Chapel where a Clarion Handicraft Exhibition was taking place, but it was closed on Sunday and the doors had been locked. Many resolutions had been submitted, but proceedings in the draughty entrance were over within minutes. The National Committee re-elected itself *en bloc* in the warmth of a nearby pub.

This was to be the last such disaster. Members had had enough of the happy-go-lucky approach to affairs. The next year (1903) in Chester there was a properly-conducted indoor Conference, and within a few more years what Blatchford had resisted came to pass – preliminary agendas, final agendas with amendments, and delegates with proper credentials. "And yet," commented Tom Groom wryly in 1915, "I hesitate to offer a record of their doings as an afternoon's amusement."

'Nunquam': Robert Blatchford, 1851-1943

(National Museum of Labour History)

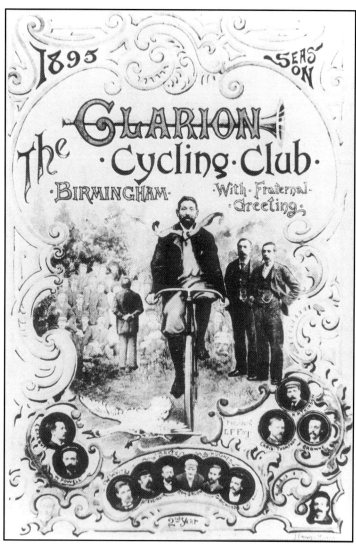

Birmingham Clarion CC Greeting Card, 1895, designed by J. Cruwys Richards (bottom right): Edward Fay ('The Bounder') on his 'Humper', Robert and Montague Blatchford standing on the right, with a back view of 'Dangle' (A.M. Thompson). Below are the faces of Tom Groom and the Committee.

(National Clarion Cycling Club)

Founder-members of Birmingham Clarion CC in 1894, photographed by one of their number, J. Cruwys Richards. Left to right: Steve Muir, W. Baker, W. Powell, Tom Groom, S. Hughes, Chris Thompson, Harry Atkinson.
(National Clarion Cycling Club)

A Clarion Van at Enfield in 1905. The speaker is Edward Hartley.
(National Museum of Labour History)

Preston Clarion CC and Band at Eddisford Bridge in May 1911.
(Derek Roberts, Fellowship of Cycling Old-Timers)

The Van built by the Glasgow Clarion Handicraft Guild, after its inauguration in Shrewsbury market-place, Easter 1914. Tom Groom, 'The Bald-Headed One', is second on the left.

(W. Alex Seaton)

One innovation in 1911 has since stood the test of time. At Warwick each member signing on and paying the Meet levy not only received a Programme for the weekend's events but also a Meet Ribbon to pin on. This was to make sure that all those attending the various functions had actually paid. The first one was simply a short piece of red ribbon printed in black with the year and place. After this a multi-coloured design was woven into the ribbons, which were produced for many years in Coventry by George Poole who was a member of the National Committee. (Eventually, financial restraints after the Second World War dictated a return to the simple printed red or yellow ribbon.)

It was probably inevitable that a more structured and formal organisation would be adopted by the National Clarion, given the steadily increasing national membership in the years leading up to the First World War. Attendances at Easter Meets reflected this growth. There were 800 at Chester in 1903 and over a thousand at each of the Meets from 1904 to 1914. The highest-ever figure was recorded at the third Chester Meet in 1910 when 1,350 signed on. In the same period national membership mounted to a peak of around 7,000 in 1913.

Shrewsbury 1914

In many ways the 20th Annual Meet in 1914, returning to Shrewsbury for the third time, saw the Clarion (as a movement, not just a cycling club) at the height of its influence and popularity. This is evident from the programme: 48 pages for threepence, illustrated with photographs, and with a design on the cover produced specially for the NCCC as a letter-head by Walter Crane the internationally-known Socialist artist. Incorporating the words "Socialism the Hope of the World", the letter-head was to be used for the next twenty years and beyond.

The 1914 Programme included a Year Book compiled by Walter Southgate of the North London CCC. Intended to be a complete record of all the Clarion organisations in 1914, it shows how the National Clarion CC, with the *Clarion* paper itself, held the movement together. As A.M. Thompson put it in 1913: "Without cycling there could be no Clarion."

The Year Book reflects the more elaborate organisational stucture of the NCCC which had developed as the national membership grew. By 1914, area sub-divisions called Unions had been established, the first in 1903 by clubs in the Manchester area. The Manchester Union consisted of 32 Sections (the term for local CCC's used since 1906.) Other areas now had similar organisations: London (17 Sections), Birmingham and District (11 Sections), North Lancashire (14 Sections), Scotland (10

Sections), Yorkshire (17 Sections), South-West Lancashire and Cheshire (9 Sections), North Midlands (9 Sections), South Midlands (7 Sections), Southern Counties (4 Sections) and Western Counties (5 Sections.) There were 10 Sections not in a Union, and a Central Section set up in 1903 for individual members not attached to a local club.

Another important development had been the introduction in 1909, after years of discussion, of an insurance scheme for members. The National Clarion Cycling Friendly Society was registered in 1912 to give members cover for accident or death while cycling. It took nearly twenty more years before the Clarion caught up with the much bigger Cyclists' Touring Club (CTC) and began to provide third-party cover and free legal advice. (By this time the insurance was being provided through the Co-operative Insurance Society.) Later still, with numbers falling, members were to be insured through the British Cycling Federation, the BCF.

After successive revisions to accommodate the organisational changes made necessary by increasing numbers, the NCCC's Constitution and Rules had arrived by 1914 at a basic form which was endure with only minor alterations and additions for another fifty years. The objects were now stated as: "Mutual aid, good fellowship and the propagation of the principles of Socialism as advocated by the *Clarion*." A majority of the National Committee was made up of representatives of the Unions in numbers proportional to their memberships. An annual national affiliation fee and membership card were specified. Sections were allowed one or more delegates to Annual Conference according to the number of members. The most controversial rule, and thus the most altered over the years, was the one which was designed to maintain Socialist control of the Club. In 1914 it said that all national officials and committee members should be "declared Socialists." In later times, after heated debate at Annual Conference, the rule stipulated that they should be members of Socialist organisations, often specifying or suggesting what these might be.

The enduring debate over this latter issue is an example of the almost continuous controversy about how active in the Socialist or Labour Movement Clarion CC members should be. Tom Groom and the six men who started it all in Birmingham in 1894 were in no doubt that the propagation of Socialism should be at the heart of their activities, but what Socialist principles were to be propagated? And what were the most effective methods to use?

PROPAGATING THE PRINCIPLES OF SOCIALISM

Chapter   Five

B y the summer of 1894, the first season of its existence, the members of Birmingham Clarion CC were discussing ideas for spreading the Socialist message when they met with their comrades in the newly-formed Potteries Club at Rugeley. Tom Groom took up the suggestion made by Nunquam in the paper a few weeks earlier: "How about a cycling corps of Clarion Scouts?" he wrote. "A pocketful of leaflets and an extra copy or two of the *Clarion* carefully left at the different stopping places may have good results."

Merrie England

It was the printing of a penny edition of Robert Blatchford's pamphlet *Merrie England* in the autumn of 1894 which gave the growing number of Clarion CCs and Scouting groups the greatest opportunity for propaganda work. A series of letters addressed to an imaginary "John Smith of Oldham, a hard-headed workman, fond of facts" had first appeared in the *Clarion* in the spring of 1892. Early in the following year the letters were put together as a shilling paperback with the title *Merrie England* and it quickly sold 20,000 copies. In August 1894 it was announced that 100,000 copies of a penny edition were to be printed at what was expected to be a small financial loss. "One gross (144) to any address in the United

MERRIE ENGLAND:

A Series of Letters on the Labour Problem.

ADDRESSED TO JOHN SMITH, OF OLDHAM, A HARD-HEADED WORKMAN, FOND OF FACTS.

By NUNQUAM.

Kingdom for ten shillings, money with order," said the announcement. Orders came in for 200,000 even before the first printing, and over 700,000 were sold within a year. (Liverpool Scouts, for example, sold 5,000 copies at an international football match played in the city.)

Eventually, two million copies were to be sold world-wide, including editions in Dutch, German, Swedish, Italian, Danish, Hebrew, Norwegian, Spanish, and Welsh.

Clarion Scouts

By the end of the cycling season in October 1894, the four Clarion Clubs formed by then were reporting their propaganda activities in the paper. Of the 25 Bradford members, 22 had formed a Scouting Corps which was doing good work in the outlying villages. Liverpool had cycled out to Knowsley on the Earl of Derby's estate. Although, as they reported, his lordship had not invited them to dinner, they supplied his tenants with *Clarion*s and Clarion leaflets. "We also called at the police station," their Secretary wrote, "and left some tracts for the edification of the gentlemen in blue." Members of the Potteries CCC, based in Hanley, had also distributed literature and claimed "the actual conversion of a few to Clarionism." And in the November local council elections both Liverpool and Bradford cyclists helped Socialist candidates in their own cities.

In the spring of 1895, so great was the enthusiasm for propaganda work that a new monthly paper was started for the activists called *The Scout – A Journal for Socialist Workers*. It was edited first by William Ranstead and then by Montague Blatchford. The first issue, in March, contained Robert Blatchford's "Instructions for Scouts", with advice about house-to-house distribution of tracts, leaflets, and the penny edition of *Merrie England*. In the factories, mines and other workplaces Scouts were urged to "permeate" their companions with Socialism, and in their own districts to form branches of the ILP or SDF where none existed already. They were encouraged to write letters to the press, ask questions at political meetings and place themselves at the service of Socialist candidates in elections. Remaining calm, polite and good-humoured, they should try always to build unity between the various organisations in the Labour Movement. The importance of the bicycle in the work of the Scouts was emphasised by the paper's editor, who suggested the compiling of a list of speakers able to cycle twenty to fifty miles on Saturdays and Sundays to address public meetings in towns and villages which had, as yet, no Socialist organisations. Cyclist supporters could paste walls and fences with stickers bearing Socialist slogans, these being obtainable from the *Clarion* Office in London.

The calling of a General Election for July 1895, in which as many as thirty Socialist candidates were expected to stand, was a powerful incentive for the Clarion CCs and Scouting groups (now over forty in number) to step up their propaganda activities. Some impression of their cheerful dedication can be gained from the Song of the Clarion Scout (words by Joseph Levy and music by Edward Pugh) which appeared in the May 1895 issue of the *Scout*:

Oh! who rides by day and night, round about
Tinkling his bicycle bell?
Hark how he nears us with laudate shout.
Hurrah! Hurrah! 'tis the Clarion Scout!
List to the story he tells.

What tho' the weather be cold as an icicle,
Bravely he clings to his Clarion bicycle
Scattering leaflets, sticking up labels,
Filling a breach at old hostelry tables.
Such is the being I'll sing you about.
Three hearty cheers for the Clarion Scout!

(Chorus):
Hurrah for the Clarion Scout!
Hail him with strenuous shout!
As bold as Lysander
To push propaganda.
Hurrah for the Clarion Scout.

Down to the haunts of the parson and squire,
Putting opponents to rout;
Bestriding his steed with pneumatic tyre,
Through village and hamlet, thro' mud and thro' mire,
Rideth the Clarion Scout

Nailing down lies and disposing of fables,
Improving the landscape by sticking up labels:
What does he care for the wind and the weather?
Be he alone or a hundred together,
He's always eager to join in a bout.
Then give three cheers for the Clarion Scout.

What do these labels mysterious teach?
What is the message they bring?
Something that comes within everyone's reach:
A gospel of Brotherhood – that's what they preach.
In praise of that gospel I sing.

They say that all produce belongs to the toiler;
To sweep from old England each idler and spoiler,
Abolish the sweater and rack-renting knave;
The land for the people – the just and the brave.
These lessons with vigour he's spreading about
Is humanity's saviour, the Clarion Scout.

Propaganda Methods

In the same issue of *The Scout* the Liverpool comrades advertised their stickers or labels. These were about four inches by two inches, printed in black on red, with the reverse side gummed. They invited suggestions from readers for new slogans, striking questions or assertions, with the word Socialism prominent. (Example: "SOCIALISM IS THE ONLY REMEDY.") They could be stuck on telephone poles, gates and walls – even, it was suggested, on the flanks of grazing cows! Also available from Liverpool were stencil plates for painting slogans – an advance on 'decorating' pavements with chalk, which could be done only on a fine, dry night.

> Objections may be raised on aesthetic grounds [wrote the Liverpool correspondent] to our methods of propaganda, but while our brothers and sisters are starving or slowly dragging out an existence of brutalising toil we cannot afford to be too nice in the methods by which we hope to effect their salvation. When we have compelled people to face the horrors of our present system, aroused their better feelings and enlisted their sympathies, we can then consider the question of taste."

The militants in Liverpool were correct in thinking that objections might be raised. The editor of the *Scout* had received complaints, and warned of the danger of prosecution for stencillers and label-stickers. If public antagonism were to be aroused, these activities would do the Socialist cause more harm than good. Nunquam had already advised 'young Socialists' only to use stickers in suitable places – not on tombstones, carriage doors, the gates of villa residences, church porches or hotel mirrors. Now it was announced that in future stickers would not be available from the *Clarion* Office, and the suggestion was made that the money of local groups would be better spent on leaflets, half a million of which had been sent out to date. Copies of the *Clarion* and *Merrie England* (now into a new threepenny edition) could be sent on approval for house-to-house sales.

A correspondent from Liverpool Fabian Society favoured this less spectacular approach to propaganda work. Tracts by Tom Mann, William Morris and Nunquam, it was suggested, could be left at houses in regular rotation, each replaced by another at the next visit. District teams of about twenty men and women were advocated, which would carry out this long-term canvassing and mark up electoral registers as a record of support. The members of such teams were advised to be "friendly, undogmatic, patient and persistent" in their approach on the doorstep.

Blatchford and the 1895 Election

The results of the work in the 1895 General Election were disappointing. Nunquam commented: "We have got rid, for a good while, of the Liberal Party. But we have got the Tory Party in its place." Four hundred Tories had been returned, and not one Socialist. Out of over two million voters only 45,000 had voted for Socialist candidates. "Scarcely any but wealthy men have got returned ... And there is hard work in front of us, and there are hard knocks in store for us. If they don't smash us during the next seven years it will not be their fault."

One man wrote to *The Scout* from Manchester that he had been appalled by the sight of poor working people wearing Liberal or Tory party colours and heatedly discussing the relative merits of their employers or exploiters standing as 'people's friends'. It seemed to him that:

> The increased application of machinery as a means of saving the payment of wages and increasing dividends and profits is displacing labour to such an extent that propertyless workers are so dispirited by enforced poverty that they have no vigour left to fight the exploiters. They have been taught to be content with poverty and its miseries by political false doctrines and unrighteous spritual advisers ... Our education system is used by capitalists to make our workers of both sexes readier machines for profit-making ... It should be the aim of Socialist missionaries in the Clarion movement to awaken workers to the ideal of a new life.

It seemed to Robert Blatchford that this ideal also needed not only a 'New Party' but a 'New Religion'. In 1892 he had summed up the Socialist programme in one essential demand: "that the land and other instruments of production shall be the common property of the people, and shall be used and governed by the people for the people". But after the 1895 General Election he moved away from political economy and towards an ethical Socialism. "To love one another as brothers and sisters," he wrote, "and to love the earth as the mother of all, that is part of our new religion [which] claims man back to freedom from commercial and industrial vassalage." From being a founder-member of Manchester ILP and an election candidate in the Bradford constituency he turned his back on parliamentary politics, writing: "We all know the great Westminster windmill where ignorant educated men grind wind with which to fill the bellies of the hapless workers." His New Party (a single united Socialist Party) would "pay no honour to selfishness, however successful, but would put the names of John Ruskin, Thomas Carlyle, Walt Whitman and Erasmus Darwin above those of all the money-spinners, fame-winners, blood-shedders and self-makers that ever encumbered the earth".

Cycling to Socialism

Although parliamentary politics interested him less and less as the 1890s went on and he increasingly left the political side of the *Clarion* to Alex Thompson, Blatchford still believed that the way forward was to 'make Socialists' through the paper and the leaflets and pamphlets it published. He saw Clarion cyclists as the "travelling prophets of a new era" – but by no means all of them were interested in this role. In the first Annual Report of the NCCC, produced by the committee of three in 1896, it had been observed that "the less direct propaganda there is undertaken by a Cycling Club, the more successful will the club be in gathering to itself members". And the secretary of Darlington CCC complained in the summer of that year that propaganda work was being prevented by members who only wanted to "ride long distances and break records". By then even the Liverpool secretary was admitting that systematic propaganda seemed "rather off" for them. "Perhaps," he reported, "this is because most of us have our noses on the grindstone of the cause six days of the week and like to enjoy the country and fresh air without being disturbed by the consideration of having a duty to perform." Meanwhile the activists, represented by the secretary of Rochdale CCC, pleaded for "propaganda, not (fancy-dress) parades," and attacked the Manchester members' "unseemly feasting and boasting".

Police Harassment

In spite of what was to be a running disagreement between members about the relative importance of political work and cycling as a sport or pastime, most of the growing number of local clubs in the 1890s regularly cycled to open-air meetings and distributed masses of literature. This required courage as well as energy, for they encountered much opposition and harrassment, not least from the police. Bristol CCC, for example, on its first-ever week-end run, held an outdoor meeting with literature selling in Bath. The police tried to move them on, but a crowd which had gathered shouted that the Clarionettes had as much right to be there as the Salvation Army. In Fareham, Comrade Rearden of Portsmouth CCC was locked up for selling *Merrie England* on the street, but he managed to persuade a police inspector and a constable to promise that they would read the copies he presented to them on his release! By contrast, when Birmingham members staged an open-air meeting in Leamington (addressed by Tom Groom and Harry Atkinson) the police sided with them, refusing the requests of respectable residents that they should intervene. Their day was slightly spoiled, though, when pubs refused to serve them on their way home, forcing them to drink pump-water in several villages.

Normally the police reaction was to threaten and then carry out arrests of the Clarion activists, using the catch-all charge of 'obstruction'. When a number of Glasgow members was arrested in a Dumbarton street for disturbing the peace by singing, about a hundred of their comrades staged a protest outside the police-station. Meanwhile, undeterred by court appearances and fines, Clarionettes up and down the country went on with the propaganda work for which their clubs were formed. Their efforts received an enormous boost when the first Clarion Van tour was organised in the spring of 1896.

WOMEN, CYCLING AND THE CLARION VANS

Chapter Six

Rock-a-bye baby, for father is near.
Mother is biking; she never is here!
Out in the park she's scorching all day
Or at some meeting is talking away!
She's the king-pin at the women's rights show,
Teaching poor husbands the way they should go!
Close then your eyes; there's dishes to do.
Rock-a-bye baby; 'tis pa sings to you.

This piece of verse, printed in the Manchester Co-operative Society's paper the *Monthly Herald* in 1898 (quoted by Jill Liddington and Jill Norris in their book *One Hand Tied Behind Us*) helps to illustrate the connection between the Women's Movement and cycling in the years between about 1890 and 1914. As Christopher Goode has observed, "The impact of cycling was at its greatest in the liberation of women."

Women and Cycling

Unlike other sports taken up by women at this time (such as badminton or tennis) cycling was not confined to the well-off, even though it was mainly the unmarried working-class women who took it up. It seems that for women of all classes, riding a bicycle symbolised their defiance of the conventional (men's) view of what was proper for them – and thus their growing independence. In their pubs and clubs, in newspaper editorials and correspondence columns, men raised the issue of women riding bicycles. Most cycling clubs in the 1880s did not admit women as members, but with the arrival of the Safety Bicycle some clubs began to let them in. The early Clarion CCs were among those welcoming women members, though sometimes not for very laudable reasons, as a (male) report from the Manchester CCC in May 1895 shows: "Lady members add a great amount of interest to our club runs and are a real source of help to us, mere men, when it comes to the inevitable tea-time."

The most frequent question asked by men about women's cycling seems to have been related to their health. It was presumed to be positively health-promoting for men, but would it not affect the functions for which women were designed by the Creator? "Every woman who rides a cycle," wrote a male cycling columnist in a local newspaper in 1897, "should understand that she can do so in moderation only and that if she attempts more she will pay for it dearly." Other questions asked in the 1890s have a more modern ring. Should a woman's bicycle, particularly its saddle, be different from those designed for men? And should a lady cyclist in distress accept help from an unknown gentleman?

Rational Dress

Perhaps the most sensational and controversial issue in womens' cycling a century ago was that of dress. Conventional styles in female attire at that time hampered movement to the extent that riding a bicycle was almost impossible, even with the skirt-guards designed to stop the entanglements in wheel-spokes which sometimes caused injury. The Campaign for Rational Dress gained fresh impetus from the cycling boom of the 1890s. 'Bloomers' (loose, baggy trousers fastening below the knee) had been worn by a few daring women since the 1850s but they now became fashionable for a minority of young women cyclists. In July 1894 the *Clarion* reported that "A great concourse of curious spectators assembles every Sunday morning near the Angel at Thames Ditton to see the New Cycling Woman in Rational Costume." Male journalists adopted a mocking tone. Swiftsure wrote in *Cycling Notes* that same summer: "A woman dressed in 'rationals' has been seen astride a machine in the Preston district. She only appeared in the dusk of the evening when naughty small boys should be asleep. Was the daring fair cyclist on her way to be photographed?"

Eleanor Keeling in *Our Woman's Column* the following spring hesitated to recommend bloomers for readers taking up cycling, merely warning against corsets and heavy skirts, and advising the wearing of vest and combinations plus a loose-fitting dress. It certainly took courage for Clarion women to wear bloomers. Bolton CCC's Sunday run was attacked in the streets of Wigan in 1897 by children ("some of advanced years," said the report) who threw stones and used pea-shooters while shouting and jeering at the one woman wearing "rationals." Yet while cycling journals were full of criticism of rational dress as "unbecoming" or "unwomanly". Swiftsure in the *Clarion* was prophetic when he wrote in 1895: "It requires no small amount of resolution to ride out in knickers, but I feel sure that in time the custom will be almost universal. It is just possible, also, that our Clarion Clubs will have a certain influence in bringing this about."

Women and the *Clarion* Paper

It has been said with some truth that Robert Blatchford was no supporter of feminism: he once complained that women did not even try to understand politics. Yet in 1895 we find him trying to make his views clear in reply to women's criticism, writing in a *Clarion* editorial:

> Women must have equal rights, political, industrial, social and civic, with men. They must cease to be chattels or vassals, or servants, or inferiors. [Man had a duty to woman:] ... to grant her at once complete freedom and complete equality, and having done that, to add as a free gift as much affection, tenderness, reverence and admiration as his rather coarse and rather selfish nature will allow.

Whatever Nunquam's own attitude, the paper he edited gave an enormous boost to the women's movement by winning thousands of female readers for Socialism and to the struggle for equal voting rights. The most influential part of the paper in this respect was *Our Woman's Letter*, written from October 1895 for the following twenty years by 'Julia Dawson' (the pen-name of Mrs D.J. Myddleton-Worrall.) It is she who must take the credit for taking up (though not inventing) a method of Socialist campaigning which was to involve thousands of Clarion cyclists during the years between 1896 and the 1920s.

The Clarion Women's Van

The idea of a touring horse-drawn caravan for spreading a political message in the countryside was pioneered by two organisations advocating common ownership of the land. The Red Van of the English

Land Restoration League and the Yellow Van of the Land Nationalisation Society were already well-known when Julia Dawson announced in the *Clarion* on 29th February 1896 a plan which she said had been taking shape in her mind for some time. It was for a thirteen-week Clarion Women's Van Tour starting in June that year. Women would tour with the Van two or three at a time; and a tent would be provided for a boy (somebody's young brother perhaps) who would volunteer to look after the horse, make fires and wash up the dishes – without wages. William Ranstead the land-owning *Clarion* writer and supporter who, like Julia Dawson, lived in Cheshire, had already offered a suitable vehicle. It had been used before on the streets of Liverpool as a Soup Van selling bowls of broth for a farthing to the poor and unemployed, as well as acting as a bill-board for posters advertising the *Clarion* and promoting Socialism. That was in the winter months, but in the previous summer it had been part of the Clarion Camp at Tabley Brook near Knutsford.

The plan was for Socialist leaflets and literature to be distributed and sold at open-air meetings held on village greens and in the market-places of small towns. Julia Dawson's appeal was for women volunteers to speak at the meetings, for the loan of a horse, and for money (about £80 initially) to buy food, fuel and equipment. If successful this could be an annual summer activity, eventually with four or five vans on the road in various parts of the country. And the Clarion cyclists would have an important part to play in supporting the vans wherever they went.

The call for money and volunteers was quickly answered. A leading Socialist speaker, Caroline Martyn, undertook to join the van for a whole month, helped by young and able workers such as Ada Nield, an elected Socialist member of the Poor Law Board of Guardians in Crewe, and Sarah Reddish and Miss Mayo of the Women's Co-operative Guild. Julia Dawson was sure that wherever they stopped, "big brothers will be there on bikes to greet the Van, and sisters will get their work done early that day to join in the gatherings". She proudly announced that this would be "the first Socialist Van ever put on the road by women".

The Van's route in the summer of 1896 was to be from Chester, where the Lone Scout, Bob Manson, and his Liverpool comrades would provide assistance; then through Shropshire, Staffordshire, Derbyshire, Lancashire and Yorkshire. The tour would finish in County Durham, where the secretary of Newcastle CCC had promised that while the Van was within a 35-mile radius of the city, regular cycling runs would be arranged so that members could help at meetings. All the other Clarion CCs in places near enough to the route were invited to do the same.

Liverpool Clarion CC announced to its members in the paper that there would be a big send-off for Julia Dawson's Van from Chester market-place at 4.30 pm on Saturday 13th June. They were asked to parade in fancy-dress for the occasion. The Liverpool Socialist Band would play, and two members of the *Clarion* Board would be present. Bob Manson, Joe ('the waggoner') O'Donnell and his son Will, a Prince's landing-stage porter in Liverpool – all three veterans of the Soup Van and the unemployed campaigns of the 1880s – would start off with the van. The Clarion cyclists would ride ahead "to herald its advent".

When the big day arrived it was sunny and warm, bringing out hundreds of supporters to cheer the Van's departure. Among the speakers who addressed the crowd before the parade moved off were the Lone Scout himself and John Edwards from Birkenhead, well-known as the editor of the *Labour Annual*. Mr and Mrs Dangle, and Mr and Mrs Candid Friend arrived on their bikes. And so the Clarion Women's Van started on its three-month journey, followed by about fifty cyclists and a huge crowd on foot, to the inspiring strains of the 'Marseillaise'.

The 1896 Van Tour

The first week, in Cheshire and Staffordshire, "left scarcely a house on the road unvisited," and everywhere on the doorstep the women and their Socialist message won a friendly reception. Clarion cyclists greeted the Van with shouts of "Boots!" before joining in the work. When the Vanners and their helpers were tired of knocking on doors they gathered round and sang the 'Red Flag' so that people would come to their doors to take the leaflets offered. When the Van reached Bridgnorth, cyclists from Birmingham (including Tom Groom) and from Wolverhampton, rode over to help out.

From the start there were problems with the planned outdoor meetings. Many of the people in country villages feared to be seen listening to Socialist speakers in case it was reported to their employers and they would be sacked – which might mean the eviction of the whole family from their tied cottage. In one place (un-named, for good reason, in the *Clarion* report) a gathering took place between 10pm and 1am by candlelight.

Bob Manson wrote to the paper about their experiences in the first week:

Notwithstanding the revolutionary sentiments emblazoned on our moving home we were never interfered with on the roadside, and were never refused leave to camp in a field ... The Clarion Van has spread the news of Socialism in a starving winter city and blossoming summer villages among tens of thousands.

In the towns the women had addressed crowds of up to 500, as at Newcastle-under-Lyme, Macclesfield and Stockport. The results of the work soon began to be reported. For example, a letter from a *Clarion* reader in Madeley, Shropshire, told of the benefits reaped in Ironbridge where a seventeen-strong branch of the ILP had been formed since the Van's visit.

After the first week the Liverpool contingent went home and back to work, all apart from Joe O'Donnell who stayed on to look after the horse Tommy (short for 'Tommy Atkins' Environment'.) From then on it was to be mainly women who did the propaganda work, with increasing numbers of Clarion cyclists riding in to help. As the Van headed north-east over the Pennines into Yorkshire it left in many places a newly-formed branch of ILP, as, for example, at Penistone. In Wakefield the Vanners stopped for five days to give Tommy a rest before sending him and the Van to Stockton by rail for the final weeks of the tour, but once in the north-east they decided to use a second horse donated by a Liverpool woman.

Caroline Martyn, the most experienced and the best-loved of the Socialist women speakers, had not been able to join the Van for the month of August as planned. In July, exhausted by her unrelenting propaganda work, she had fallen ill in Dundee and died there – a tragic loss to the movement. Within weeks Julia Dawson was asking in the *Clarion* for donations to provide another Van – bigger, but lighter in weight. This would be named in Caroline Martyn's memory, while the original vehicle would be called the Clarion Pioneer Van.

The tour went on, with daily meetings addressed by women like Ada Nield. She had been relatively inexperienced in public speaking before joining the Van, but had rapidly gained the confidence to address the crowds of up to 2,000 which assembled in the larger towns like Sunderland and South Shields. The help given by the Clarion cyclists became indispensable, and their clubs also gained members when ILP branches were formed. The tour ended on 23rd September 1896 after fifteen weeks of hard work covering six counties.

Van Tours 1897-1914

The Caroline Martyn Memorial Van made its first appearance outside St.George's Hall in Liverpool on 1st June 1897 before a crowd estimated at over a thousand, many of them Clarion CC members who had cycled into the city from a wide area. The Van was then sent by rail to Bristol where the second annual tour was to start. This took the Socialist message into South Wales where the pattern of 1896 was repeated, the Van leaving in its wake not only new ILP branches, as in Newport and Monmouth, but also Clarion Cycling Clubs and Vocal Unions (choirs).

It was not easy work; local councils, employers and landowners in several places tried to disrupt the Vanners' activities. Sites for the Van and for meetings were refused, as at Abergavenny. An open-air meeting in Thornbury was broken up by the police at the instigation of local farmers and collections had to be taken up to pay the fines of those prosecuted.

The same story, with the same results, continued through the remainder of the decade and on into the new century. In 1902 the Caroline Martyn Van went over the border into Scotland for the first time "in a new dress of green and gold", as Julia Dawson put it. The old Pioneer Van ended up a wreck in St.Annes-on Sea on the Lancashire coast, having been used for a number of years as part of a summer camp for poor children. It was replaced by Van No.3, later named after J. Taylor Clarke of Stalybridge who had become the first real Clarion CC National Secretary in 1900. Responsibility for raising funds and organising Van tours passed in 1902 from Julia Dawson to Edward Hartley of Bradford, and by 1907 the number of Vans had been increased to six. One (the 'William Morris') was in permanent use for the London area, and another (the 'E.F. Fay') for the Midlands. London had acquired its second Van by 1909 with the additional one named after Enid Stacy, another important Socialist woman lecturer. During 1911 the Vans held a total of 400 meetings covering 88 districts countrywide. Two years later the *Clarion* paper's Board announced that they could no longer accept responsibility for raising the money to finance the work of the Vans, and after the issue had been debated at the York Easter Meet the Clarion CC's National Committee agreed to take over. By 1913 it was clear that the NCCC was by far the strongest of the Clarion organisations; as Alex Thompson wrote in the paper, "Without the cycling there could be no Clarion."

Tom Groom, now National Secretary, proposed that the NCCC should aim to build and maintain three Vans, these to be designed by Walter Crane, "our well-known and excellent friend". Constructed of oak, they were to be horse-drawn (a motorised Midlands van had proved unreliable.) In addition to these Vans it was envisaged that the Lancashire, Yorkshire and Scottish Unions of the National Clarion CC should each provide their own.

On Easter Sunday 1914 at the Annual Meet in Shrewsbury, a new Clarion Van was inaugurated in the town square by Robert Blatchford. Chairing the ceremony was Fred Hagger of London, newly-elected as National Van Secretary, while the Potteries Clarion Vocal Union sang Glees. A widely-sold postcard photograph shows the magnificence of the new Van, its sides and interior decorated with panelling carved by members of the Glasgow Clarion Handicraft Guild. It was put to use that summer by the Manchester Union, and in the following year by the North Lancashire Union.

There can be no doubt that the Clarion cyclists had played an essential role since 1896 in helping to make the work of the Vans effective; mainly by distributing Socialist literature and forming the nucleus of an audience for outdoor meetings, but also by contributing much of the money needed. Over two decades, thousands of people had been influenced by the Vanners' political message, many of them helping to found branches of the ILP. In addition, the Van tours had given initial experience in public speaking to dozens of men and women who were to devote their lives to the cause of Socialism or to the Women's Movement.

CLARION CAMPS AND CLUBHOUSES

Chapter   Seven

The idea of a residential country clubhouse for Clarionettes, both cyclists and non-cyclists, grew out of a summer camp in 1895 organised by two Manchester CCC members: C.D. (Charlie) Reekie and J.D. Sutcliffe. 'The O'Reekie', a frequent correspondent in the *Clarion*'s cycling columns, worked as a railway clerk, lived in Ancoats, Manchester, and was a talented amateur entertainer with his comic songs, humorous recitations and 'lantern' slide shows. Sutcliffe ('The Cheery One') was the proprietor of an industrial heating and ventilating firm in Manchester and had acted as secretary of the three-man National Clarion CC committee elected at the first Easter Meet in Ashbourne.

The Tabley Camp 1895-96

For the camp's headquarters Sutcliffe borrowed a caravan from his fellow committee member William Ranstead, who had been one of the *Clarion*'s original Board, having contributed some money to start it up. He farmed near Malpas in Cheshire. It was, of course, the famous caravan which had been used on the streets of Liverpool the previous winter as a Soup Van and which was to be the first Clarion propaganda van the following summer.

Sutcliffe and Reekie hired some tents and a horse said to be "as quiet as a lamb but a devil to go". They found a stove and borrowed tables, benches and crockery from the Gorton ILP rooms. After a very slow day's journey from Manchester they pitched a marquee and three bell-tents in a field they had rented at Tabley Brook near Knutsford.

Over a period of three weeks in August 1895 the camp was visited by some 2,000 cyclists. More than 400 slept there at sixpence a night, and about 1,400 meals were served, costing ninepence or a shilling per head. In Charlie Reekie's words, the camp provided "comradeship and fresh air at reasonable cost". He wrote a little verse about it:

Where thrushes sing and the busy bee hums,
Far from the stinking, stifling slums,
We'll pitch our tents by a troutling stream,
Sink all sorrow, nor think of the morrow,
But look on life as a happy dream."

The following August there were fourteen bell-tents and two marquees in a bigger field nearby, attracting even more Clarionettes in spite of poor weather. Tom Groom wrote later: "We were six weeks under canvas – and not one fine week-end!" Auld Reekie summed it up again in the *Clarion*:

The rugs are wet and the beds are damp,
Conducive to ague, rheumatic and cramp.
We're praying for sunshine,
But the weather gets wuss,
Causing the campers to quietly kuss.

Bucklow Hill 1897-1903

Charlie Reekie was already dreaming of a permanent country Club House, his inspiration the Guest Houses described by William Morris in *News From Nowhere*. The original plan was to rent a cottage and land within half a day's ride of the South Lancashire towns which had established Clarion Cycling Clubs. Next to the cottage they would erect a timber pavilion with sleeping bunks.

In the spring of 1897 the Clarion Cyclists' Club House Company Limited was set up in Manchester after an appeal for support to members and friends in the north-west. The purpose was the renting of the house named Acropolis at Bucklow Hill near Knutsford, for the "refreshment, recreation and accommodation at reasonable cost" of Clarionettes from Bolton, Liverpool, Manchester and surrounding towns. The Company's Prospectus offered shares at five shillings each, repayable at a future date, but with any profits to go to the Cinderella Fund for poor children, or similar work. Described as the "first Socialist Guest House", and an "experimental co-operative cottage of the Clarion Clubs", Acropolis was to be leased, for five years at the outset, from the local landowner. Among the promoters of the scheme were: Robert Blatchford, his brother Montague, A.M. Thompson, and Emmeline and Richard Pankhurst.

The Clubhouse was opened on 22nd June 1897, a public holiday for Queen Victoria's Diamond Jubilee. By July it was already winning the enthusiastic approval of visitors. One described it as "the centre of a cycling paradise, away from the smoky towns." Another told of hilarious Saturday night concerts in a large marquee. These went on into the early hours, to be followed by cycle rides to local beauty spots on Sunday morning. Cycling journalists described the Clubhouse and its grounds in some detail for their readers after being invited to sample its delights. On the lawns outside they found deck-chairs under gay Chinese umbrellas where people were taking a siesta or reading. Nearby there was an orchard with apple, pear and cherry trees, and a pond with water-lilies. A marquee and a number of bell-tents were pitched in the adjoining field, which had space for rounders, cricket and football. There was secure accommodation in the stables for bicycles, and inside the house itself, a large kitchen, a dining-room, an office and a library/reading-room. Upstairs a lounge opened on to a balcony. The dormitories, described as "airy", each contained five single beds, and were named after flowers. A total of 150 people could sit down in the marquee and dining-room to eat a mid-day meal costing a shilling, while a bed indoors cost ninepence a night (outside in a shared tent, sixpence).

Clarion cyclists from Liverpool, Manchester and the Lancashire mill-towns needed no convincing of the Club House's merits. Looking back in later years, one of them (Collin Coates) wrote:

> To be able to wheel out on a Saturday or Sunday after the week's toil and moil in the dingy office, the stuffy warehouse, the reeking slum, the enervating mill, workshop or mine – to one's own house ... which was the rendezvous of kindred souls bubbling over with the spirit of the newly-found Fellowship, was indeed a taste of the joys to be had in the 'days-a-coming.'

Another old Clarionette recalled "the utter absence of Sabbatarianism, class distinction and moth-eaten convention which characterised life at Bucklow Hill". Yet these words show why some local people did not approve of what went on at the Club House. They complained to the landowner, Lord Egerton of Tatton Hall, who had not realised that Acropolis had been let to Socialists. When the lease expired in 1902, he refused to renew it, so the Clubhouse was forced to find another location. A vacant farmhouse was found about eight miles away to the east, still in Cheshire, amid the fields near Handforth.

Handforth 1903-1936

The rambling old building had oak beams and panelling inside. There was a sitting-room, a kitchen, and a room which was made into a library, well-stocked with books – especially Clarion Press publications.

The four dormitories held a total of fifty beds, and there were tents to sleep at least a dozen more outside in the summer. "Fresh-air fiends," said a publicity brochure, "can always be accommodated with a blanket in the haystack." Eventually wooden outbuildings constructed by Clarion volunteers provided a dining-room to seat 200, and a billiard-room.

One of a series of coloured postcards sold at the Clubhouse shows a well-kept garden with a lawn and wooden benches. Fruit and vegetables were grown in a kitchen garden and orchard. Another of the picture postcards shows a second orchard which was used as an open-air theatre or auditorium. Beyond the gardens and orchards was a large playing-field with three tennis courts, plus football and cricket pitches.

The Handforth brochure outlined the aims of the second Clarion Cyclists' Clubhouse as: "Co-operation for pleasure, intellectual recreation and interchange of opinions and ideas." Maintenance work and 'artistic service' were contributed voluntarily by members. Although it was officially the country headquarters of the Manchester Union of the National Clarion Cycling Club (the first regional Union to be set up, in 1903) it catered for large numbers of people who came from all parts of the country, either on bikes or by train, tram and bus. Members of Socialist organisations could join at a lower fee than the 'unattached', who had to be vouched for by an existing member.

Mabel and Collin Coates were Manchester Clarion cyclists until they emigrated to Australia in 1912. Sixty years later Collin remembered the early days at Handforth in words which could have been echoed by thousands of men and women:

> The Clubhouse became a sort of pivotal centre, and no matter where our wheels had led during the day, always would they turn towards Handforth by evening. 'Clubhouse for tea' became a sort of slogan ... There were amongst the members at that time many who were able and willing to draw from their store of talents: singers, players, reciters could always be tapped to provide good entertainment. Weather permitting, concerts were arranged in the orchard. On the 'stage' beneath the pear-trees the artists did their stuff. What a quaint collection of characters were drawn to the Clarion movement. Artists, doctors, lawyers rubbed shoulders with miners and little-piecers, all linked by the common ideal and their faith in Socialism.

Menston: 1908 to the Present

The Clubhouse idea was eagerly adopted in other parts of the country by Clarionettes who had sampled the delights of Bucklow Hill and Handforth. Bradford CCC members started an annual camp in Wharfedale in the late 1890s: five second-hand bell-tents in a field between Otley and Burley, where cycle runs went every Sunday for a month or more in the summer. By 1906 Bradford's annual camp had changed its site several times, but then the newly-formed Yorkshire Union of Clarion CCs began to look for a permanent 'countryhouse'. Early in 1907 the Yorkshire Clarion Clubhouse Ltd was registered as an Industrial and Provident Society offering supporters half-crown shares. The aim was to build a 'Bungalow Clubhouse' for £200 in some convenient centre in Wharfedale. The following year they took a three-year lease on one of their previous camp sites, a four acre field at Chevin End near the village of Menston. There was an option to purchase outright, but they needed to raise a total of £500 to make this possible.

At first they made do with tents, and then they put up ramshackle sheds and lean-tos until they had gathered enough money from the half-crown shares to have a proper Clubhouse built in stone. Even then they had to proceed slowly, adding architect-designed wings as funds became available. Next to the Clubhouse, while leaving space for camping, volunteers levelled the ground for tennis courts and made a 'carriage-drive' planted on both sides with forest trees. Soon, a separate two-storey timber building had to be erected to provide forty more beds. Sadly,the latter was later razed to the ground by fire, but the stone buildings remain to this day as the only proudly-surviving Clarion Clubhouse, used still by Clarion cyclists and others.

Ribble Valley 1913-1950s

In 1913, another north-west Clubhouse opened at Clayton-le-Dale, near Ribchester in Lancashire. This boasted more extensive grounds than any other. The Ribble Valley Clarion Clubhouse Ltd had gained the support of about 600 shareholders in the North Lancashire Union of the NCCC, mainly from the Blackburn and Preston areas. An estate of nearly twenty acres and a spacious house belonging to the Duke of Somerset were purchased freehold at auction for about £750.

On 15th June 1913 more than 2,000 people attended the opening ceremony to hear speeches by Robert Blatchford and Tom Groom before wandering through fields and woods on the banks of the River Ribble. The Clubhouse itself could accommodate about 120 in the dining-room at one sitting, though sleeping space indoors was limited and bell-tents had to be pitched on busy summer week-ends. There was ample space for cricket and football, and once the undulating land had been levelled, tennis courts and putting greens were laid out.

Halewood: Nazeing: Lyndon End

Other Clubhouses were started in the years before the first world war. Liverpool opened one at Halewood in 1907, but it had closed by 1912. Most of them began as camps, like the one near Romford in Essex which became the London Clarion Clubhouse. Offering members an escape from the "smoke and turmoil of the Metropolis," it was opened at Whitsun 1913 in the hamlet of Broadley Common near Nazeing after a permanent building had been secured. It lasted only until 1920.

The first Midlands Clubhouse was opened on 27th February 1915 at Lyndon End, Yardley, Birmingham, with a dinner to celebrate the 21st birthday of the first Clarion Cycling Club. Four of the original seven were there, with twenty more who had joined in the first year, and 200 other Clarionettes.

'For t'Fellowship'

In a 21st Anniversary Supplement published with the *Clarion* in 1912, Tom Groom related a story to illustrate the basic principle of voluntary co-operation upon which the Clubhouses had been founded. It was about an upper-class, non-Clarion visitor to a northern clubhouse:

> "What," asked the Superior Person after he'd watched the men scraping potatoes and washing greens, and then handing round the meals to the hungry crowd of Clarionettes assembled, "What is the precise pecuniary remuneration of these persons?"
> "What's their which?" demanded the comrade.
> "I mean," said the Superior One, "what do they get for this?"
> "They get nowt, lad," replied the comrade, "unless something goes wrong, and then they get jip."
> "Then," said the Superior One, "why do they do it?"
> "They do it for t'fellowship o'course," answered the comrade. "What else does ta think?"

THE CLARION MOVEMENT 1894-1914:
A NEW WAY OF LIFE

Chapter
Eight

For large numbers of *Clarion* readers, its apparently non-political features were the most important. All the various cultural, social and leisure activities promoted in its columns offered a complete way of life outside the toil and drabness of the world of work and crowded urban living. Indeed, the Clarion movement in its first two decades can be seen as an attempt to pre-figure life under Socialism as William Morris had seen it before his death in 1896. And the weekly paper, with its announcements and reports, was essential in enabling Clarion organisations to get started and maintain their existence in the localities.

In addition to cycling, which gained the biggest following, the main activities before the first world war were choral singing and rambling (the latter combined with nature-study.) All the activities were, to a greater or lesser extent, connected with Socialist propaganda work. And they tended to overlap, so that cyclists, choirs and ramblers often met up at the same Saturday or Sunday afternoon venue.

Clarion Music

The Clarion Vocal Unions (CVUs), and the Socialist Choirs and Bands, started at about the same time as the Cycling Clubs. Concerts (or 'smokers') were the main social events aimed at keeping members together during the winter months when the weather discouraged weekend outings. And no decent-sized Socialist public meeting was complete without musical items.

The first mention of a choral group in the paper came in the autumn of 1894 when, to wind up their inaugural cycling season, the Birmingham and Potteries CCCs held a joint social evening in 'Brum'. Their favourite *Clarion* writer, Edward Fay (the Bounder) was invited, and, specially for the event, some members of the Potteries Club formed a Glee Party or small choir. Within a few months Hull Clarion Glee Club had followed their lead and Clarion music-making was under way. By the middle of 1895 more than a dozen of these choirs had been formed, and Montague Blatchford had become leader of the Clarion Vocal Union movement nationally. His stated object was "to encourage unaccompanied vocal music [performed] creditably and with understanding". By far the biggest local group was in his hometown, Halifax, where by 1895 there were 146 members plus an 'elementary class' of 48, and an orchestra. The average weekly attendance for rehearsals was 120, when Mont Blong was teacher and conductor.

It was in South Lancashire and the West Riding of Yorkshire that the CVUs, like the Cycling Clubs, took deepest root; and soon they were eager to arrange inter-club meets. Hardcastle Crags, a beauty-spot near Hebden Bridge in Yorkshire, not far from the border with Lancashire, became a regular venue for CVU picnics and outdoor concerts. At the first of these gatherings, on Saturday 1st June 1895, there were present about a hundred Clarion members, with 150 relatives and friends. Many came on their bikes, proudly wearing the new silver badges pinned in their caps. The mixture, according to the report in the paper, was of "sandwiches, laughter, tea, tobacco and singing". There was also a thunderstorm, followed by a rain-soaked dash to the railway station where songs echoed round the platforms as they waited for their trains home.

Liverpool had a Socialist Brass Band which practised every Wednesday night in preparation for performances at indoor and outdoor public meetings. ("There's nothing like sweet music and singing to draw the people," a *Clarion* writer once commented.) Glasgow and Bristol both had choirs by 1896, when national CVU membership reached 1,250. The second Hardcastle Crags Meet that year attracted more than 2,000 people to listen to massed choirs on the hillside, and speeches by Caroline Martyn and Keir Hardie.

In May 1899 the first CVU United Concert at the Free Trade Hall in Manchester took place, with 450 singers in fourteen choirs competing for the ivory and gold Challenge Baton which had been presented by the *Clarion* Board. This was to be an annual event for the next thirty years, bringing hundreds of Clarionettes to Manchester, cyclists and non-cyclists alike.

Songs were specially written (like the Song of the Clarion Scout) and poems were set to music to form an extensive Socialist repertoire. Young composers and musicians were drawn to the cause, like Gustav Holst, who was a regular cyclist and often rode with his trombone strung across his back. While studying at the Royal College of Music and living in a bed-sitter in Hammersmith, Holst became the first conductor of the Socialist Choir there. He wrote reports for the *Clarion* about the choir, one of whose members was his future wife Isobel. Holst's fellow-student, Rutland Boughton, set poems by William Morris to music, and they appeared in the *Clarion Song Book* published in 1906.

Field Clubs and Rambling

Clarion Field Clubs first emerged in 1895. Their aim, as announced in *The Scout* by Harry Lowerison, an elementary school teacher in the East End of London, was "to diffuse a love and knowledge of the animal and plant life of the fields, of the old-time remains left to us, of folk-lore, and generally of the outdoor world". The idea for the Clubs sprang out of what he described as "a revolt ... from the sordid ugliness of modern competitive, commercial life". Members' interests, he suggested, might include: flowers, insects, birds, fossils, trees, geology, botany, archaeology and astronomy. Field Clubs would support the work of protecting animals and birds, and preserving the commons and footpaths, and ancient buildings. The main activity would be to conduct Saturday afternoon or Sunday rambles during which short papers might be read in the open air.

As with the Cycling Clubs and Vocal Unions, progress in forming Field Clubs was rapid at first, especially in the Clarion heartlands of Lancashire and Yorkshire. Lowerison's own Club in London had an even broader view of relevant activities than his. One of their early rambles included a reading by members of the forest scene from Shakespeare's *As You Like It*; and on another of their outings William Morris himself gave a 'forest chat' following some open-air singing.

Harry Lowerison saw *Clarion* readers as a united fellowship, whatever their particular leisure interests. "Cyclists, glee folk, Scouts, Clarionettes all, buy the badge and wear it," was his call in the paper, and he advised that on every cycle run there should be at least one Field Club member. Better still, the cyclists should meet up with the 'field folk' at an agreed weekend destination.

Some Socialist activists were critical of the Field Clubs for the lack of political content in their programmes, but Lowerison saw no reason to apologise, claiming that: "We shall do our work a thousand times better for a hearty laugh, and still better for a genuine rest occasionally." In any case, he argued, "the best fruit of our rambles is not knowledge of nature, nor even closer touch with and deeper love for her beauties, but simply human comradeship."

Clarion Field Clubs were never to be as numerous as the Cycling Clubs, but by 1897, in addition to those in Lancashire and Yorkshire, in

North Staffs, Glasgow and Edinburgh, there were three in London. Here, winter activities included talks on subjects ranging from Ibsen's plays to economics, visits to concerts, museums and galleries – and dancing classes! New groups were still being formed in 1898; the Socialist Rambling Club in Derby, for instance, where members aimed to discuss Socialist literature as well as natural history on their walks.

Though these Clarion Clubs were far less successful than those for cyclists, their members claimed that there were distinct advantages in expeditions on foot. You could avoid the high roads and what one writer to the paper referred to as "the white dust of the motor's rush". It was admitted, however, that you might have to break fences and "tear down the trespass boards" to gain access to the countryside.

The 1914 *National Clarion CC Year Book* had a section headed "Ramblers", which shows that by then many of the Field Clubs which had flourished in the 1890s were no longer in existence. A notable exception was the one in Sheffield which had been started by Herbert H. Stansfield of the Norton Socialist Colony in 1895. It was re-founded by G.H.B. Ward as Sheffield Clarion Ramblers in 1900, and was said in 1914 to be the biggest rambling club in the country with 470 members. It continued to thrive after the first world war, but lost touch with the rest of the Clarion movement after the 1920s.

Swimming – And More

Clarionettes were often keen to compete against each other in a range of physical activities and pastimes. Newcastle-upon-Tyne and London had Clarion Swimming Clubs in 1896, and Oldham, Bradford and Liverpool led the way in the north of England. Aberdeen and Glasgow were the first in Scotland. By the early years of this century there were enough to form a National Clarion Swimming Club with its own silk woven badge to sew on costumes. (National Swimming teams were to compete abroad in the 1920s as part of the International Workers' Sports movement, though cycling and football were pre-eminent.) The 1914 *NCCC Year Book* also listed gymnastics, cricket, billiards, hockey and tennis clubs, all associated mainly with the Clarion Clubhouses.

Dramatic Societies

Between 1900 and 1914 groups of Clarion Players or Dramatic Societies were established in about a dozen places up and down the country, with two purposes: the development of dramatic art, and the propagation of Socialist ideas. In 1910, ten such groups were brought together in the Clarion Players' Union. "We realise," wrote the National Secretary, Norman Veitch, in 1914, "that most good art is good propaganda, so that in an indirect manner we express, through the drama, the living truths of Socialism to people who otherwise are never touched by the ordinary methods of street-corner meetings and manifestoes." Not surprisingly, Shaw's plays tended to dominate production lists, but Ibsen and Shakespeare were also tackled. Any surplus from money taken at the box office was used either to assist propaganda work or the Cinderella Fund for poor children.

Camera Clubs

The Clarion Camera Club made its appearance as early as 1895, organised initially by J.Cruwys Richards, one of the seven founder-members of Birmingham Clarion CC. He rightly suggested that photography could very happily be combined with cycling or rambling. By the 1890s cameras were much cheaper and more portable than they had been earlier in the century, and they could be a very useful adjunct to political work. For example, lantern slides could be produced illustrating social inequalities, and these shown as an addition to speakers at public meetings. In some places, as at the Handforth Clubhouse, darkroom facilities and instruction in photographic techniques were offered to Clarionettes. In 1896 William Palmer (Whiffly Puncto of the *Clarion*) toured the country with his slide show, advertised in the paper as "The Greatest Show on Earth – The Famous Clarion Limelight Lecture: Merrie England – It Will Wreck the Government and Inaugurate the Social Revolution."

Handicraft Guilds

Clarion Handicraft Guilds were formed following a suggestion by Julia Dawson in her *Woman's Letter* in 1901. One such group announced itself in the paper as: "Artistic craftsmen and women making furniture sound in construction, beautiful in form, moderate in price." "The designs," said the advertisement, "are distinctive, refined and unusual, and are based on a return to Nature as the true source of inspiration for artistic effort. All profits go to the Workers!"

Handicraft Exhibitions were staged at the National Clarion CC's Easter Meets, where (in addition to furniture) metalwork, jewellery, fabrics and footwear were displayed for sale "at prices which give the craftsman a fair return for his labour, but no exorbitant and unearned profits to middleman or landlord".

The Clarion Fellowship

Clarion readers did not have to be keen on cycling, singing, rambling, or any of the other specific leisure interest clubs or groups, in order to meet up with others who shared their Socialist faith. Clarion Fellowship Clubs existed in many towns and cities in the early 1900s, and the Fellowship held its own separate conferences at the National Clarion Cycling Club's Easter Meet.

The movement had its own social centres, usually called clubrooms, which complemented the cyclists' country clubhouses. These were to be found in a number of places by 1900, including Derby, Leeds, Glasgow and North London. A Clarion Cafe, run by the Lone Scout, Bob Manson, opened before the turn of the century in Williamson Street, Liverpool. This did not remain in business as long as the one in Market Street, Manchester, which started in 1908 and was notable for its William Morris and Walter Crane furnishings and decor. It was still in existence in the 1940s.

A national constitution for the Fellowship was adopted at the Bakewell Easter Meet in 1901. Members wore a distinctive badge: a small red enamel crescent (or 'C' for Clarion) on a silver pin or trumpet. Groups of this "comradely confraternity", as one member described the Fellowship, continued to meet until well after the end of the second world war. From the beginning the main purposes were social: eating, drinking, but above all, talking. The Clarion Fellowship's slogan was once given as: "The propagation of the principles of Socialism – and leave politics to them as likes 'em!"

BLATCHFORD, WAR AND THE PAPER'S DECLINE

Chapter   Nine

Robert Blatchford himself must bear much of the blame for the decline of the *Clarion* after 1914. As early as 1897 he had been criticised by readers for what some saw as his 'jingoism', or nationalistic militarism. He defended himself eloquently against these charges, but when British troops embarked for South Africa to fight the Boers of the Transvaal in 1899 he came out in defiant support for the war. To the consternation of Socialists who opposed what was for them the Tory government's imperialist aggression, he declared:

> I cannot go with those Socialists whose sympathies are with the enemy. My whole heart is with the British troops ... I regard all those who have taken arms against England as enemies to be fought and beaten ... My daughter has orders to play *Rule Britannia* every night while the war lasts.

Many *Clarion* readers were incensed. As his biographer, Laurence Thompson (Alex's son) wrote: "In Labour Clubs and Labour Churches Blatchford's portrait was taken from the wall and solemnly consigned to outer darkness. An ebullient Clarionette, Bob Manson of Liverpool, painted a great black cross over his picture of the prophet Nunquam." Hundreds of Socialists stopped buying the paper, even though so many articles were printed supporting the Boers that it was banned by the British authorities in South Africa.

After this there was an even wider gulf than before between Blatchford and many in the Labour movement. He despised the new federally-organised Labour Party formed in 1900, and had never been on friendly terms with its leaders, Keir Hardie and Ramsay MacDonald. Yet once the Boer War was over, he and the paper recovered much of their former popularity, so that when 29 Labour MPs were elected in 1906, he claimed (with some justification) that the *Clarion* and *Merrie England* had played an important part in what he described as "an astonishing revolution".

The British Socialist Party

Robert Blatchford did not rate Labour politicians very highly as Socialists under his definition, so when the young Victor Grayson won a famous parliamentary by-election victory at Colne Valley on the Lancashire-Yorkshire border in 1907, Blatchford hailed him as "the first Socialist MP", joining him on a speaking tour which attracted packed audiences that autumn. Grayson lost his seat at the 1910 General Election, by which time Nunquam had once again completely lost faith in politics and politicians. Forty Labour MPs had been elected this time, but Alex Thompson returned to London after a trip north to find that the *Clarion* was about to come out without a word concerning the election. His friend Robert had hardly noticed it was taking place!

It was at this time that Victor Grayson, together with other *Clarion* supporters, SDF members and dissident ILP-ers, revived the idea of a new Socialist Party. In 1911 Tom Groom represented the National Clarion Cycling Club at a conference in Salford which set up the British Socialist Party. The BSP received strong support from the *Clarion* in the years that followed.

Nunquam and the First World War

Blatchford, however, in his own words "tired and disappointed", had already retreated to a cottage at Heacham on the Norfolk coast near the Ruskin School Home run by his friend Harry Lowerison. He was once again in disgrace with many in the Clarion movement for writing articles in the Tory *Daily Mail*. He had been warning of the "German menace" ever since 1904, and in 1910 had called for the strengthening of the army and navy to defend the British Empire. Some saw the *Daily Mail* articles as "selling out" to the Tories, and at the Chester Easter Meet that year Blatchford was booed and hissed at the Sunday night concert by Clarionettes who had once idolised Nunquam. Undeterred, he went on to advocate on the front page of the *Clarion* the compulsory conscription of young men into the armed forces, while still avowing his belief in Socialism. And although he temporarily turned against conscription again when troops were used to break strikes in the period of industrial unrest which preceded the outbreak of war in 1914, he returned to the theme once the fighting had started in France. "Conscription on British lines, and only for the period of the war, will have to be adopted if, after a thorough trial the voluntary system fails us," he wrote early in 1915.

Alex Thompson, now editing the *Clarion*, quickly noticed the effects of the war (and particularly Blatchford's stance) on the circulation of the paper. Tom Groom, still National Secretary, told him that the voluntary enlistment of *Clarion* readers (many into the Army Cyclist Corps) had made great gaps in the membership of the Cycling Club's local Sections. Thompson himself admitted "a very perceptible effect upon circulation" – in fact, a rapid drop from around 60,000 to no more than 10,000. A 'Maintenance Fund' was started, while the size and number of pages were reduced.

When conscription was eventually introduced by the government in 1916, Blatchford redoubled his criticism of pacifists. He viciously attacked those Socialists who became conscientious objectors, many of whom suffered harsh imprisonment, or even died as a result of their treatment. Pacifist Socialists like Fenner Brockway had for him "no right to exist upon the planet at all". He believed that Socialism should now be shelved for the duration of hostilities. Collin Coates wrote many years after:

We could not square Socialism, as we had understood it, with the organised killing of others of our own class. This attitude aroused Blatchford to a pitch of patriotic fervour which caused him to abuse and vilify such of us as had failed to drop our Socialism for a narrow nationalism. Even Alex Thompson (Dangle) added his little quota and coined the elegant term 'sloshialist' for attachment to those who did not toe the popular line – not a very clever use of his talents. The *Clarion* came out full of letters purporting to have been received from 'conchies', 'malevolents', 'defeatists' etc. They must have been very carefully culled for their ineffectuality and stupidity, as they were without exception well below the standard one would have expected from the average 'objector', and certainly none were included of the quality that many must have been. Only the easily answered arguments were dealt with; anything of telling force, or anything unanswerable except by evasion or complete abandonment of all that the *Clarion* had taught, was never given space.

All this really ended the Movement as it had been; schism set in, and the 'good fellowship' which had ruled turned sour. 'Workers of the World Unite' no longer had any meaning; we were now 'British' or 'German', or, worse, 'pro-Germans', 'malignants' – anything the reverse of 'nice.' All the invective the Staff could think up was heaped on the heads of those who were doing no more than act in conformity with RB's advice to 'think for yourselves!'

Two of Bolton Clarion's 'fast lads', Teddy Grant and George Barr, in 1930s time-trialling garb: black alpaca jackets and legs covered.

(Bolton Clarion Cycling Club)

The Yorkshire Clarion Clubhouse at Chevin End, near Menston – established in 1908 and still going strong.

(The author)

Workers' Olympiad, Prague, 1927: the British (Clarion) Cycling Team in the opening parade.

(National Clarion Cycling Club)

Workers' Olympiad, Antwerp, 1937: the British Workers' Sports Association team which came third in the 50km time trial. Left to right: Jack Mullineux (Bolton Clarion), Bill Grundy (Lincoln Clarion), Charlie Damyon (Woolwich CC).

(Jack Mullineux)

A Clarion anti-fascist demonstration, about 1936. (Notice that some of the 'worker sportsmen' are women!)
(National Clarion Cycling Club)

Happy days! Bolton Clarion women at the start of a Sunday run in 1939.
(Bolton Clarion Cycling Club)

1984: Bolton Clarion members before the start of a sponsored ride to support the families of Lancashire miners on strike. (Author, far left.)

(Bolton Socialist Club)

2002: Oakhill Clarion's Charles Jepson (National Secretary from 2003) and Ruth Coates on their End-to-End ride.

(Charles Jepson)

In the summer of 1916 Robert Blatchford and Sally, now living at Horsham in Sussex, received the devastating news that their son, Corri, had been killed whilst on active service with the British Army in Flanders. (He was the third of their five children to die, two having been lost through illness in the 1880s.) The mass slaughter of the "Great War To End Wars" must have affected hundreds of Clarion families. The 1917 Easter Meet at Buxton was abandoned soon after it started, and only the Annual Conference of the NCCC was held the following year, in the same town. As Tom Groom later explained: "War and its casualties made it impossible to hold junketings."

Resolutions submitted to the 1918 Conference show that the National Clarion CC, like other Socialist organisations, was split in its attitude to the war. Manchester and Glasgow Sections were successful in having the words "as advocated by the *Clarion*" deleted from the end of the statement of aims in the Rules, which was also printed on the national membership card, to leave just: "Mutual Aid, Good Fellowship and the Propagation of the Principles of Socialism." Crewe Section protested against "the present attitude of the *Clarion* with regard to its policy on the war". Burnley Section, on the other hand, wanted to "endorse the official position of the *Clarion* in regard to the war". The National Committee expressed its sympathy with the relatives and friends of members who had died in what was termed "this titanic conflict", and sent greetings to those who were serving in the naval and military forces.

Death of the Paper

After the war, with Thompson and Blatchford still at the helm, the *Clarion* struggled on as a smaller-format, twelve or sixteen-page weekly, selling at threepence. Its circulation dwindled still further as many Socialist activists, influenced by the revolution in Russia, turned to Lenin, Stalin, Trotsky, and the newly-formed Communist Party of Great Britain. Blatchford admitted in his autobiography *My Eighty Years* that one CPGB member had called him: "the world's greatest traitor, and the traitor most accursed". His view of the Communists was that: "There ought not to be such a thing as poverty in any civilized country, and though the policy of the Reds is wrong, their impatience is pardonable and natural."

In the spring of 1927 Blatchford and Thompson gave up their control of the *Clarion*, which then became a sixpenny monthly edited by W. Arthur Peacock. RB, AMT and Tom Groom continued to contribute, and the paper maintained its political line of supporting a Labour movement "as opposed to Trotsky as it is to Mussolini ... as opposed to Bolshevism as it is to Fascism". To Alex Thompson the *Clarion* was a casualty of the war. He complained bitterly in the 36th Birthday issue in 1927 that in its effects of ruining the paper and of "destroying the golden harvest of the seed it had sown," the 'Great Catastrophe' seemed to have wiped out very effectively any interest which may have lingered round the paper's history. He himself, with Nunquam and the rest of the Board, had "simply loved England and the English people, while hating slums and poverty". Their goal had been the Co-operative Commonwealth, but "the submerged class, whose misery we had hoped to mend, never supported us at all".

Now an "independent monthly Socialist review", the *Clarion* (and the *New Clarion* which succeeded it in 1932) failed to maintain a viable circulation, despite the contributions of such notable writers as Robert Graves, H.E. Bates and J.B. Priestley. In 1934 the paper disappeared completely, 'merged' with a new pictorial weekly magazine, the *Illustrated*.

The Second Clarion Cycling Boom

Paradoxically, the demise of the *Clarion* coincided with a dramatic increase in the membership of the National Clarion Cycling Club. Between 1933 and 1934 it rose from 2,693 to 4,330 according to the Annual Report, with the number of local Sections up from 104 to 146. The growth continued, until membership reached an all-time peak of 8,306 (with 233 local Sections) in 1936.

Clearly, it was something other than enthusiasm for what had been the Clarion's brand of Socialism which boosted the Cycling Club's fortunes in the 1930s. One favourable influence was the craze in that decade for getting out into the fresh air of the countryside at weekends in organised groups, whether of hikers, ramblers or cyclists. There had been a similar open-air movement in the 1890s and early 1900s, but between the first and second world wars, despite recession, depression and unemployment, a bike, either new on hire purchase or second-hand, came within the financial grasp of a far greater proportion of the population. Most manual workers used a bike to travel to work every day, even though many in white-collar, salaried jobs were beginning to find a small car within their means. There were probably about ten million cycles on the road compared with only one million cars, as cycling clubs proliferated in the 1930s. And Clarion members were not just interested in weekend runs and touring; an increasing proportion of them, mainly young men (but some young women), had become enthusiasts for competitive cycling on road and track.

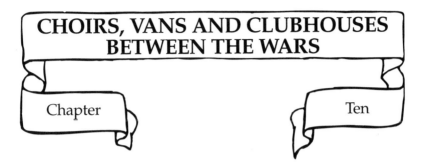

CHOIRS, VANS AND CLUBHOUSES BETWEEN THE WARS

Chapter Ten

While cycle sport and anti-war, anti-fascist activity took centre-stage with many Clarion CC members between 1918 and 1939, the activities which had established a Clarion culture before 1914 remained, though for some of them there was a gradual decline.

Vocal Unions

In the 1920s, despite the *Clarion*'s falling circulation, the Vocal Unions still attracted good support. The annual contest was continued, and even though the number of choirs dwindled in the 1930s, concerts in places like Oldham and Rochdale were still popular events. The outdoor gathering at Hardcastle Crags near Hebden Bridge went on throughout the inter-war years. The second Sunday in July became known as Clarion Sunday, and was well described by Jack Eastwood, a stalwart of Bolton Clarion CC, in one of his regular reports for the local paper in the 1920s:

> Sunday last was eventful in more ways than one. First, the thermometer read 110 in the sun; second, it was the annual July meet of the Clarion Cycle Club held at Hardcastle Crags. In spite of the intense heat prevailing during the day, close on 400 cyclists attended. The members of the various Vocal Unions, operating from the beautiful green sward 'neath the shadow of the bold Hardcastle Crags, enthralled us with their rendering of tuneful airs.

The Last of the Vans

When peace came in 1918 the Vans had resumed their work, despite a creeping loss of enthusiasm for political activity among Clarion cyclists as interest in racing increased. Vans toured in the London area, and in Derbyshire, Lancashire and Yorkshire in the early 1920s. In 1927 a

Clarion Van was used by the Labour Party for its agricultural campaign in Lincolnshire, and it was on the road again in the 1929 General Election campaign. It was supported this time by the Lancashire and Yorkshire Unions of the NCCC, and contributed to the election of the second minority Labour government of the decade.

The 1929 Van tour proved to be the last. At the 1930 Easter Meet in Buxton, when rain and snow reduced attendance to just 457, it was agreed that the Vans had completed their work. The Labour Party was in government, with more MPs in the House of Commons (287) than ever before. Every part of the country had its local Labour Party (600 of them), many owing their foundation to Clarion Van visits in the heady pre-1914 years.

Tom Groom was not at all happy with the state of the movement, asking in the *Clarion* (by now a monthly) whether the Cycling Club was about to "die of wasting sickness". But his fears about falling membership proved groundless: the numbers grew spectacularly in the mid-1930s. And Tom became more concerned with developing what he called "international fraternity" through the medium of sport than with the propagation of Socialist principles at home.

After what was seen by many as Ramsay MacDonald's 'great betrayal' as Labour Prime Minister, when he formed a National Government with Tory support amid an economic crisis in 1931, there seemed for some in the NCCC to be a greater need than ever to revive the work of the Vans. But the last spark was extinguished in 1933 when a Clarion 'campaign lorry' finished its run from Oxford to Bristol.

Clubhouse Revival

The Clubhouses had struggled to stay open during the 1914-18 war. Many members were on active service, and there were additional problems caused by food shortages and high prices. But when peace came there was an eagerly awaited revival of their fortunes.

By 1920 the Midlands Clubhouse had moved to a building in Wagon Lane, Sheldon, Birmingham. It was big enough to have a large hall for parties and dances, as well as sleeping accommodation, It remained open until the early 1930s.

The members of Sheffield Clarion CC had run a camp-site in the Cordwell Valley, Derbyshire, for many years until they managed to raise £420 in one-pound shares to buy eleven acres of land and erect a timber building near Dore, on the Hathersage Road five miles out of Sheffield. The Clubhouse opened in 1920 – the same year as yet another one in the north-west.

At Tottington, near Bury, about 700 people turned up (thirty or forty on motor-cycles!) to celebrate the opening of the South East Lancashire Clubhouse. They listened to Tom Groom and other speakers before marvelling at the way in which the dilapidated shell of a house had been converted into a comfortable building. There were now six residential Clubhouses, and their representatives gathered at Tottington for a conference in November 1920.

From 1927 to 1932 an annual Inter-Clubhouse Sports meeting was held, usually at Handforth or the Ribble Valley – but once, in 1929, at Sheldon, not long before it closed. There also existed for a few years in the early 1930s an Affliated Clubhouses Committee for mutual assistance.

As well supporting the larger Clubhouses, many Clarion CCs and Sections since the 1890s had maintained small non-residential social centres for longer or shorter periods of time – like the one run by Liverpool members at Burton, on the Wirral, in the 1930s and '40s. These came and went, too numerous to mention individually.

By 1939 there remained only three of the Clubhouses which, in the years before 1914, had been the fore-runners of youth hostels and holiday camps: those in Yorkshire (at Chevin End, Menston), in Lancashire (near Ribchester) and in Cheshire (not far from Styal.) The last of these was the successor to Bucklow Hill and Handforth, which had pioneered the Clubhouse idea. The move from Handforth had taken place in 1936 after housing development at Heald Green overtook the Manchester Union's best-loved country home. Valley House, with its four acres of land on the banks of the River Bollin at Oversley Ford, gave a new generation of Clarion cyclists in the north-west the chance to enjoy the tradition of good fellowship before the outbreak of a second world war.

Home-from-home for Manchester Clarionettes

THE NATIONAL CLARION AND CYCLE RACING

Chapter   Eleven

The *Clarion* began to report cycle racing in the summer of 1893 as part of a *Pastimes* page which had been dominated up to then by news of cricket and football – though with some rugby, boxing, hockey, tennis and swimming added. After this, the page continued to include brief items about cycling events; and when the first Clarion Cycling Clubs were formed in 1894 and 1895 their members quickly became involved in cycle sport.

Manchester Clarion CC seems to have been the first to organise racing events. Only a few weeks after the Club's formation in January 1895, they were planning a 25-mile track handicap for members. At about the same time, the Potteries Clarion CC reported that they had lost one or two of the "scorching fraternity" to other clubs because the club did not encourage participation in racing. Some degree of conflict between the more competitive and the more social-minded or Socialist members was to exist for the next hundred years, and more.

Manchester Clarion continued to set the pace. In Whit-week 1895 at the start of their first season, social runs were cancelled to facilitate the staging of one-mile and ten-mile track (or 'path') events, with gold badges for the winners.

Other Clarion CCs were opposed in principle to such activities. The 'Premier' Club, Birmingham, joined their local NCU centre, but objected when they were asked to become involved in competition. A letter was sent to protest about "the large amount of attention paid by them (the NCU) to racing matters".

Belle Vue Sports and Scottish Carnivals

In August 1898 the Manchester Club organised the first of their annual race meetings (or Sports) at Belle Vue. The editors of the *Clarion* had donated a silver cup to be awarded to the winning four-man team in a five-mile track race. The Clarion Cup would be held outright by the

Clarion CC which provided the winning team in three consecutive years. A dozen clubs entered, as well as the Manchester hosts; they included: Nottingham, Stockport, Liverpool, Rochdale and Oldham. The outcome was that Nottingham and Rochdale tied as winners and held the cup for six months each. Another event in this first Belle Vue Sports (which drew a total of 148 entries) was a ten-mile handicap, with the winner's gold medal donated by the cycle manufacturers Rudge-Whitworth. In this male-dominated age there was only one event for women – a Ladies' Slow Bicycle Race. There was no protest from feminists: indeed, the Sports had been organised by a woman – Mrs. Leeming.

Manchester's successful promotion encouraged Glasgow Clarion to stage their own version in August 1900 on Celtic Park's concrete track. After five years the event was moved to the rival Rangers FC stadium, Ibrox. The money raised by charging for admission and selling programmes at these Scottish Athletic and Cycling Carnivals went to the Glasgow Clarion Cinderella for their work with poor children.

By 1914 the Belle Vue Sports had become a national event. Invitations were issued to all Unions and Sections in the country, urging members to come as spectators and enjoy the fellowship, or to compete for the various prizes, cups and shields offered to winners in both cycling and athletics. The number of women's events had increased, and there were children's races in which the 'bitterness of defeat' was to be sweetened by giving each entrant a prize.

So popular was racing with members of the Manchester Section by this time that it was thought important to ensure that everybody should take part in social activities as well. Rule 14 stipulated that: "Before members are eligible to compete for prizes in the Sports, Races or Time-Trials, they must have attended Saturday or Sunday runs for six week-ends of the current season, in addition to having completed twelve months membership."

Time-Trialling Between the Wars

After the 1914-18 war and through the 1920s and 30s racing became increasingly important for young men joining the Clarion. In 1920 when national membership climbed to over 3,000 again, Tom Groom remarked in his cycling column on the "striking post-war development of road-racing". This meant individual time-trials, mainly over 25 or 50 mile courses. Mass-start races on the road were illegal in Britain, though not on the Continent. Time-trials took place in semi-secrecy, with courses specified only by letter and number, with the riders dressed in black alpaca from the neck down to wrists and ankles. Times were slow in comparison with those recorded today. In 1920, for example, the Manchester Union 25-mile time-trial was won by H.Williamson in 1 hour, 11 minutes, 30 seconds. But enthusiasm knew no bounds as Clarion Sections up and down the country organised both club and open events.

Sunday runs, though still considered of prime importance, were too slow for the hard-riding racing men, who often formed their own 'Speed Sections' within the clubs. Tom Groom and the National Committee were concerned about this development, suggesting in 1924 an extra insurance premium for members of the 'speed packs' being formed, and recommending that the 'fast lads' should join the rest of the club at the tea destination on Sundays to ride home with them.

By the end of the 1920s, annual National Clarion 25 and 50 mile time-trials were being suggested as Easter Meet events. The first time-trial at an Easter Meet had, in fact, taken place at Shrewsbury in 1922, but was not repeated until 1928 when Shrewsbury was again the venue. Sadly, it was the death of a young Birmingham member which brought about a regular Annual Meet time-trial – a '25', with a trophy for the fastest aggregate time by a three-man Section team. Kenneth Humphreys (son of Hubert, who went on to become a Labour Alderman and Lord Mayor of Birmingham) was killed in a crash while riding his motor-cycle to the Handforth Clubhouse on Christmas Day in 1927. Donations flooded in for a Memorial Trophy, which was first won by South-East London Section at the 1929 Chester Meet with an aggregate time of 3 hours, 34 minutes, 34 seconds. (The Kenneth Humphreys Cup has been presented every year since then, and the aggregate times are now under three hours.)

Clarion Racing Organisation and National Championships

At the 1930 Conference during the Buxton Easter Meet, the NCCC elected its first National Racing Secretary: Tommy Hirst of Blackburn. He was dedicated to what he described as the "clean, amateur competition" of time-trialling, "a game for men of grit", with no tactics, crowds or nationalistic rivalry as on the Continent. At the York Meet in 1932 Tommy was given an elected National Racing Committee, and the following year at Nottingham it was decided to give the racing members in each Union their independence in Clarion Cycling and Athletic Clubs (C.& A.Cs). At the same Conference, following a successful Bolton Section resolution the year before, it was decided to award prizes to the members amassing most points during the year for performances in 25, 50 and 100 mile time-trials, and in track events. The first to be awarded the Vaughton Cup as National Road Champion was

Gilbert Hamilton of Glasgow; and the first National Track Champion was Donald Dove of Huddersfield. Both received gold medals.

As the only workers' cycling club, the Clarion was appointed by the Trades Union Congress in 1934 to organise racing events celebrating the centenary of the Tolpuddle Martyrs' defiance of anti-Trade Union laws. The following year's Easter Meet at Shrewsbury saw the first conference of C.& A.Cs, and by 1936 each of the Unions had its own C.& A.C. Centre affiliated to the Roads Racing Council, fore-runner of the Road Time Trials Council, the RTTC.

Cycle Sport and Socialism

In 1939 the National Racing Secretary, Alex Taylor of the Springburn (Glasgow) Section, was able to write proudly in the *Clarion's* National Bike Week publication, under the heading "The Clarion At Speed", of the Club's rapid progress in time-trialling. There were now half-a-dozen "top-liners" in the Clarion, and it was no longer merely a "nursery" for other clubs. As an example, he cited his brother Jack Taylor, who was Scotland's current Best All-Rounder (BAR Champion) and holder of more than one Scottish open record. Though the Clarion had no big names on the track, its annual Fallowfield track meeting in Manchester (formerly the Belle Vue Sports, but transferred from there in 1930) had built up a national reputation.

Alex Taylor refused, as some members would have wished, to separate Clarion cycle sport from Socialism:

Our biggest asset [he wrote] lies in our being a working-class organisation. When a rider competes in the Clarion name, the success of that rider reflects credit on the Clarion, and this indirectly helps the Clarion cause of Socialism ... The knowledge that he is riding for a principle ... gives new energy to tired legs.

His brother Jack added his own endorsement of Socialism:

I am proud to ride for the Clarion because I believe that the propagation of Socialism should still be the main object of the Club, especially in these days of crisis following crisis, when the weaknesses of our present capitalistic system are becoming so glaringly apparent.

The Taylor brothers were exceptional: it is much more difficult to find a connection between Socialism and cycle-racing within Britain than in international competition. Tom Groom since 1913 had done more than anyone else in this country to encourage the development of the Workers' Sports movement, which aimed to promote international working-class solidarity and prevent another catastrophic world war.

PEACE THROUGH SPORT: THE CLARION CC AGAINST WAR AND FASCISM

Chapter   Twelve

A t the end of 1912 the French Socialist Sports Federation invited the National Clarion Cycling Club to send representatives to an international conference of Socialist Physical Education Groups to be held in Ghent, Belgium, on 10th May 1913. Tom Groom, National Secretary, and Fred Hagger, a London member of the National Committee famed for his work with the Vans, were appointed as delegates. Tom and his wife Nancy cycled all the way ("barring that bit across the Channel," he wrote later). Fred travelled by train and boat, and they met up in Ghent. In the conference hall they listened to long speeches in French, German and Italian - not understanding a word. They left before the end. Later they heard that an International Workers' Sports organisation had been set up. Tom had been elected to the Committee, which was to meet in Brussels later in the year. Despite continuing language problems, he learned in Brussels that a constitution for the International Socialist Sports Federation had been drawn up, and that the affiliation fee for each country was to be £2-10s (£2-50p). The next international conference was fixed for Frankfurt in September 1914 – but war broke out before it met.

The Lucerne International 1920

With peace in 1918 came a determination on the part of many British and European Socialists involved in sport that never again would workers of different countries be persuaded or compelled to slaughter each other at the behest of national governments with their oppressive economic and political systems. "Peace Through Sport" was to be the slogan of the revived movement in the 1920s and 30s. The International was re-formed at Seraing, Belgium, in 1919, when it was agreed that the Germans should be invited to join again. The National Clarion, representing Britain, was invited to take a football team, plus cyclists, runners and swimmers, to France, Belgium, Austria, Germany and

Czechoslovakia. The first post-war Congress of the International took place at Lucerne in Switzerland the following year. Tom Groom, who had been driven to the edge of despair by the carnage of war and the bitterness of the division between pro- and anti-war Socialists, wrote in the *Clarion*: "We have started the international movement as a contribution towards the protection of nations against future war."

No longer National Secretary of the Clarion CC, Tom devoted himself to the work of promoting the Workers' Sports movement in Britain and on the Continent. The awkwardly-named International Union for Workers' Physical Education and Sport set up a Central Bureau in Brussels. Its objects stated that the organisation was for Socialist youth of both sexes who were fighting against capitalism, and that it aimed to develop in them the taste for, and the practice of, physical education, sports, gymnastics, cycle-racing and cycle-touring. Sinking all previous antagonisms, it was hoped that they would strive towards international peace through anti-militarist action. Young workers were called on to leave 'bourgeois' athletic organisations and join their efforts with other Socialists "to hasten the triumph of our common ideal".

Tom Groom had misgivings about the approach of some other Socialists, once commenting: "I never did understand how universal brotherhood was to be brought about by preaching a class war." Nevertheless, he had no objection to echoing the call "Workers of the World Unite" early in 1921 when the International Union was embarking on what he described as "a special attempt to use the sporting instincts of the workers as a means of breaking down international prejudices". At the same time he advocated the learning of the international language Esperanto to reinforce progress towards breaking down misunderstanding between people of different countries and "killing the war spirit".

'Footballs, Not Cannonballs!'

Tom set about raising the necessary money to bring a football team from the Labour Sports Federation in France to the 1921 Easter Meet at Chester to play against a Clarion team. The match was played on Chester FC's ground, and the ceremonial kick-off was performed by the veteran Socialist H.M. Hyndman wearing his famous top-hat! In 1922 the Clarion team played a return fixture in Paris, and it was hoped that a triangular tournament would take place at the 1923 Easter Meet in Buxton. In the event, insufficient money was raised, despite Tom's efforts. Instead, a French team played a Clarion and Labour team in London on Easter Monday, the French winning 2-1. These matches were promoted under the slogan "Footballs, Not Cannonballs" as part of what was described in the *Clarion* as "a new movement towards international peace by substituting sport for militarism".

Workers' Olympiads in the 1920s

The most spectacular workers' sports events in the inter-war years were the Olympiads held in various European cities. A preliminary effort took place in Prague in 1921, when the Clarion team, representing Britain, brought home a massive bronze statuette – now awarded annually, as the Czechoslovakia Trophy, to the winning Pursuit team at the National Clarion Track Championships. It took three more years of preparation before the first Workers' Olympiad proper could be staged in Frankfurt in the summer of 1925, although teams of Clarion cyclists, footballers and swimmers had toured France, Belgium and Germany in the intervening years. When 1925 came, only enough money had been raised to support a squad of six cyclists, Britain's sole representatives among thousands of worker-sportsmen and sportswomen. Between them, the six Clarion men took part in eight events, gaining four second places and three thirds. Another Czech Olympiad at Prague in 1927 again saw the Clarion cyclists (accompanied by Tom Groom and Clarion National Secretary Ernest Sugden) as the only British team. In the mass-start road-race they took the first four places in a field of 39.

Workers' Sports in Britain

In addition to his efforts to raise money through his *Cyclorama* column in the *Clarion* so that teams could compete abroad, Tom Groom worked hard in the 1920s to persuade the Trade Unions and the Labour Party to support the organisation of the Workers' Sports movement in Britain. Before the Frankfurt Olympiad in 1925 he wrote an article for the ILP paper *New Leader* in which he argued that "whether this country will be adequately represented depends on whether the Labour Party and Trade Unions are wise enough to recognise the great value of the movement as a means of maintaining international peace". Above all, he wanted their help in organising a British Workers' Sports Federation which would be a Section of the International set up by the Lucerne Congress. Such a federation had, in fact, been started in 1923, but being Communist-dominated, was not granted recognition by Labour and the TUC. Fresh hopes were raised in 1927 when the TUC was won over and a national workers' sports conference seemed in prospect, given Labour Party support – but this was withheld.

The BWSF had affiliated to the Red Sports International, the rival Communist body to the one set up in Lucerne. Trouble blew up in 1928 when two men, Hill and May, were expelled from the Lucerne-affiliated National Clarion CC for competing in that year's Red Workers' Spartakiade in Moscow. (Hill, a member of the Barnoldswick Section in North Lancashire, was later to be reinstated after promising not to re-offend.) Meanwhile, George Bennett of the Clarion CC's London Union made some headway with the Labour Party in the capital. A Festival of Labour was staged at the Crystal Palace in the summer of 1928, and it included sports events. George was elected Secretary of the Sports Committee for the Festival, and used this as a springboard for the formation later that year of a London Labour Sports Association, of which he also became Secretary.

Bennett added his voice to Tom Groom's in calling for a Labour-supported workers' sports organisation in Britain which could add one more to the rapidly increasing number of affiliations to the Lucerne International. They went on arguing that a "new rivalry in sport" could replace the "old rivalry of war". In the meantime, workers' sports activists abroad valued highly the existing British affiliation, even though it was only that of the National Clarion CC. One of the Clarion's delegates to the Fifth Congress in Prague of the IWSF in 1929 (Jack Deveney of the Levenshulme Section in Manchester) reported: "They firmly believe that we are much stronger in number than we are."

In 1930 a National Workers' Sports Association was at long last constituted, with George Bennett as Secretary. Tom Groom expressed his satisfaction:

> Now those of us who have been hammering away at the notion of international peace through sport since 1913 have always recog-nised that until the Trade Union movement and the Labour Party came in with support, there was no hope of succeeding ... That interest has been aroused, and there's every likelihood of success.

Vienna 1931

Fund-raising began in earnest to send Clarion cyclists as part of a British NWSA team to the Second International Workers' Olympiad to be held in Vienna in 1931. A team of six (out of a total of 28 British competitors) set off, accompanied by the National Clarion Secretary, Ernest Sugden, and Jack Deveney. The team was: Colin Copeland and Frank Johnson (of the Oldham Section), Tommy Hirst (Blackburn), Ernest Deveney (East Manchester), James Tattersall (Heywood), and Frank Miller (Goldthorpe). About fifty other Clarionettes travelled as supporters.

The Clarion team emerged from the Olympiad with one winner: Colin Copeland in the 20km track race. (He also achieved second place in the 1km sprint.) Britain came fourth overall out of the 21 countries which sent teams. Tom Groom had raised £136 to pay the expenses of the Clarion team – £4 short of his target – but he immediately set about trying to make up the deficit, and to raise more money for the next Prague Olympiad, set for 1934.

Divisions Within the Workers' Sports Movement and the Clarion

There was now a widening rift between the British Workers' Sports Federation (affiliated to the Red International) and the Lucerne-affiliated National Workers' Sports Association. In 1931 a BWSF team took part in the Red Spartakiade games in Berlin, and went on to compete in Russia the following year. This split in the workers' sports movement was reflected within the membership of the National Clarion.

In April 1930 a Midlands-based left-wing Socialist group had started to produce a monthly paper, *The Clarion Cyclist*, which came out for twelve issues. This caused rows both in the National Committee, and at the Easter Meet Conferences in Buxton (1930) and Warwick (1931). The paper was virulently opposed to the Cyclists' Touring Club (the CTC) which then, as now, was by far the biggest national organisation for cyclists. The CTC was attacked for claiming to be non-political when, in the words of *Clarion Cyclist*, it "glorifies capitalism and religion by electing kings and landowners as its patrons and presidents". It was further accused of trying to "poison the minds of the workers". An editorial in the October 1930 issue explained:

> Cycling is daily becoming more popular and it is our duty as members of the working-class to build up the Clarion Cycling Club so that at least one sport will be under the control of the workers and thus cut out the harmful capitalist propaganda carried out in our fellow-cyclists' ranks by such tools of the capitalists as the CTC.

The writers and editors of the *Clarion Cyclist* took the same un-

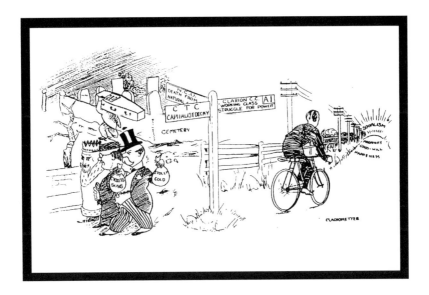

compromising line over international workers' sport. They supported the BWSF as the British Section of the Red Sports International and praised the organisation of their Spartakiade games, where: "Instead of competitors taking part as Englishmen or Frenchmen, Germans or Russians, they assemble as workers, and instead of the blatant challenges of the various national anthems, the song which stirs the pulses of the Socialist sportsmen and women is the International."

The Lucerne International, to which the National Clarion was affiliated, and which had banned any contact with the BWSF, was accused of betraying the Socialist cause and the working-class in 1914 by "failing to lead European workers in a general strike against the war". Clarionettes were invited to follow the example of the expelled members, Hill and May, and defy the "Lucerne dictators" by competing in the Red Spartakiade.

It was the BWSF which organised the international sports festival at Dorchester in 1934 to mark the centenary of the sentencing of the Tollpuddle farmworkers to transportation for organising a trade union. Teams of cyclists and athletes came from Czechoslovakia, Belgium, and Switzerland, as well as Palestine; and Clarion cyclists won the 25-mile time-trial and the hill-climb.

Against Fascism and War

The rise of the Nazi movement in Germany which brought Hitler to power, and the invasion of Abyssinia by Fascist Italy under Mussolini made international Socialist solidarity even more crucial for Clarion members. At the 1936 Easter Meet in Chester a 200-strong Annual Conference condemned the staging of the Olympic Games in Berlin that summer. The resolution declared:

> Fascist Germany, by racial discrimination and religious and political persecution has aroused the horror and contempt of the sportsmen of the whole world. This Conference calls for the transfer of the Games to another capital and refuses to participate in any Games in Hitler Germany.

Another resolution, supported by a vote of 120 to 71, stated that "The NCCC refuses to support any capitalist war, whether organised by an Imperialist British Government or the League of Nations." The Conference also decided to organise 'anti-war activity' on the occasion of the Annual Service at the Cyclists' War Memorial in Meriden, Warwickshire, held since 1921 to remember cyclists killed in the war. The activity was to take the form of an open-air meeting addressed by 'Kuklos' (Fitzwalter Wray), a much-respected cycling writer in the *Daily Herald* who was both a Socialist and a pacifist. For its part, the British (formerly National) Workers' Sports Association tried to force the executive of the Amateur Athletics Association to call a special meeting to discuss a British boycott of the Berlin Games, but the motion was defeated.

The Spanish Civil War

In Spain, in the summer of 1936, a People's Olympiad was being organised in Barcelona. It was aimed towards "giving a lead to youth to suppress fascism and war". Jack Taylor, a member of the Clarion's Kinning Park Section in Glasgow, was picked to lead a team of five cyclists to Spain. But the People's Olympiad never started. Civil war between the Republican government and Franco's fascist forces broke out on the day following the arrival of the Clarion team. They left for home, as did most of the other competitors, leaving only a few to join the thousands of foreign volunteers who fought the fascists.

In September 1936 at a meeting in the Menston Clubhouse the Clarion National Committee put on record its view of events in Spain, affirming its solidarity with Spanish workers "in their fight against the menace of fascism and reaction that has caused incalculable suffering and hardship". The resolution called on the British government to withdraw what was seen as its support for the fascist rebels through its ban on the supply of arms to the legitimate and democratic Spanish Republic. The Labour and Socialist Movement was urged to prevent 'leakages' of arms to the fascists by setting up Vigilance Committees which would, if necessary, call on transport workers to strike against the handling of war materials destined for Franco's troops.

At the Durham Easter Meet in 1937, delegates to the National Clarion Conference moved from the anti-war position of the previous year to support for the volunteer International Brigade fighting on the Republican side in Spain. A resolution saluted the Spanish people in their "heroic fight for freedom against the forces of international fascism", and mourned the deaths of two Clarion members who had been killed in action with the International Brigade near Madrid. Roy Cox (who had been Secretary of the Southern Counties Union) and Tom Durban were just two of the many who had met death in defence of democracy and freedom. The resolution ended: "Recognising that fascism destroys liberty for sportsmen, and that its only use for sport is to harness it to militarism, Conference pledges to actively help all anti-fascist forces at home and abroad." A sum of twenty guineas was voted to be divided between the Spanish Medical Aid Committee and the International Brigade.

Antwerp 1937

The Third International Workers' Olympiad had been fixed for Antwerp in July 1937, and the BWSA had agreed that the British cycling team would be supplied by the National Clarion. United in opposition to the fascist threat, the Durham Conference had urged the BWSA to persuade the Lucerne International to allow Red Sports International members to attend.

It was intended that the Clarion cycling team should consist of six track and six road competitors, but problems arose with the sport's ruling body, the National Cyclists' Union. The NCU, like the Amateur Athletics Association with its track and field athletes, threatened to ban from future competition any cyclist who took part in the Antwerp Olympiad. They said that the event was 'political' (unlike the Berlin Olympic Games the year before!). Because of this interference, a greatly reduced number of BWSA teams took part – in football, tennis, table-tennis, chess, and cycling.

In the 50km Time-Trial, the British cycling team, made up of Jack Mullineux (Bolton Clarion), Bill Grundy (Lincoln Clarion) and Charlie Damyon (Woolwich CC), came a creditable third. The same three, together with Eric Heath (Aston Section), the National Clarion Racing Secretary, took part in the 140km road-race on a closed circuit the following day. They were at a great disadvantage compared with the other riders since they had no experience of the tactics of mass-start road races, for long illegal in Britain. All four abandoned before the finish, but Jack Mullineux gained special praise for being the last to climb off at 70km. (Jack, a cotton-worker in Bolton in the 1930s, recalled that he forfeited a week's wages to compete in Antwerp, and that his trade union paid travel and hotel expenses.)

Rotterdam 1938

The National Clarion's agonised concern about the fascist threat to European peace was reflected again in the Conference resolutions passed at the Gloucester Easter Meet in 1938. The British government's support for the Non-Intervention Pact, also signed by Germany and Italy, was condemned as 'farcical' in view of the involvement of Hitler's and Mussolini's forces on the side of Franco's fascists in Spain. Later that year £136 was raised by Clarion cyclists for the Spanish Medical Aid Fund through a sponsored relay ride from Glasgow to Barcelona.

The last Workers' Olympiad took place in Rotterdam in the summer of 1938, but the Clarion was not represented. Once again the NCU withheld its approval, preventing Alex Taylor, the National Racing Secretary, from obtaining the necessary international permits. A team of four had been chosen for the 50-mile road-race: Jack Taylor and W. Mowat (West of Scotland C.& A.C.), Jack Mullineux (Manchester C.& A.C.) and Bill Grundy from the Lincoln Section – but they never set out. The Clarion National Committee reacted by threatening to discontinue the Clarion's affiliation to the BWSA because it had not taken adequate steps to try to get the NCU's ban lifted. It was thought that the BWSA should, as a member of the Lucerne International, have been able to persuade them to negotiate an agreement with the UCI, the body controlling international cycling competition.

Second World War

By Easter 1939 Franco's fascists had defeated the Republican forces and their Socialist volunteers from abroad. At the Annual Meet in York the assembled Clarionettes mourned the loss of all those (including more than 500 from Britain) who had been killed resisting them. At the Conference Harold Lamb, Secretary of the Stretford (Manchester) Section, successfully moved a resolution for a collection be taken over the week-end for the International Brigade Memorial Fund.

Although war against Germany and Italy now seemed inevitable, the Clarion National Committee declared itself opposed to the introduction of conscription for military service. It criticised the government's failure in the past to collaborate with Soviet Russia, France and the USA in halting Hitler's aggression without war, and pledged itself to work for the defeat of the Prime Minister, Neville Chamberlain. It was already too late. After the shock of the Nazi-Soviet non-aggression pact in August 1939, Britain's declaration of war soon followed. Tom Groom's hopes of securing Peace Through Sport were finally dashed when the second world war of his lifetime broke out on September 3rd.

Tom's immediate response was to try to make sure that the National Clarion CC was kept intact for the duration of hostilities, and that members serving in the forces were kept in touch. At the Buxton Easter Meet in 1940 a Conference motion condemning the war as an 'imperialist adventure' was defeated, but by then many Clarion members were already in uniform. With brave words about hopes for a speedy peace, the writer of the Meet Programme (probably the National Secretary Ernest Sugden) reflected that those who had been called up would be present in spirit, and proposed that the Meet be dedicated to those called away to fight.

AFTER TOM GROOM: THE NATIONAL CLARION'S SECOND HALF-CENTURY

Chapter   Thirteen

The Club maintained its existence during the second world war, just as Tom Groom had been determined it would in 1939. With so many people uprooted from their homes by war service of all kinds, national membership fell below 2,000 and never rose above 3,000 until peace came in 1945. Members serving in the forces were kept in touch with their clubmates at home in various ways. The Bolton Section, for example, collected money from members still at home to send weekly postal orders to those away. The Manchester Union monthly paper *The Trumpet*, started by Tom White of the Levenshulme Section in 1943, was posted to members on active service, and they wrote letters back to be used in a section of the paper titled *Forces' Notes*. Harold Lamb of Stretford, for example, who fought in Burma, once wrote from India to tell readers how he had been cycling on a hired machine and had been reduced to walking back to camp after nine punctures in succession!

1944 Jubilee

The Easter Meet took place every year during the war, though numbers were so reduced in 1941 that Valley House (the Manchester Clubhouse) was able to accommodate everybody. The 1944 Meet in Buxton celebrated the fiftieth anniversary of the formation of the first Clarion CC in Birmingham. A special luncheon was arranged at the Ashwood Park Hotel with Tom Groom, now billing himself as "the last of the First Seven", as the main speaker. Tom also wrote most of the Jubilee Souvenir which was published in time for the Meet. In this short history of the Club which had been his life, he looked forward to the peace which was not far away:

> When this war is over the need for, and the still greater possibilities of, linking up in friendly rivalry the Workers of all countries on the

field of sport, will be evident to every Clarion cyclist. It will be our duty, and our pleasure, to strengthen in every way the efforts of the BWSA, and to take our place in the new endeavour to substitute the sanity of sport for the madness of murder.

Tom's postscript to the Jubilee Souvenir was one of his last messages to Clarion members. He died on Sunday 15th July 1945 at the age of 74:

Of all the Clarion organisations which were formed fifty years ago the Clarion Cycling Club alone remains fully alive. And so long as it keeps true to its Objects: Mutual Aid, Good Fellowship and the Propagation of the Principles of Socialism, it will have good cause and reason for keeping alive. Boots!

The Tom Groom Trophy

For Tom, the NCCC without its Socialist basis was hardly worth preserving. In another piece written towards the end of his life (in the April 1944 issue of *The Trumpet*), he had stressed again that "It was cycling and Socialism which made the Clarion CC." And he had reminded readers that in the early years "A Clarion CC which existed merely for cycling was considered a very poor thing indeed."

A Tom Groom Memorial Fund was started in 1946 to provide an inscribed plaque at Golders Green where his funeral took place, and also a silver trophy. The latter was completed in 1949 at a cost of £120. (Now, it would probably be valued at over £5,000). It is in the form of a globe, which spins, and is engraved with geographical accuracy. The arm which stretches around the sphere to hold its axes carries the words: "Socialism, the Hope of the World." The Trophy is awarded annually to the Section which has, in the words of the Rule, "given the most meritorious service to the National Club". Leicester Section was the first to receive it in 1949.

Tom's devotion to the Socialist sports movement was reflected after his death in the National Clarion's continued affiliation to the British Workers Sports Association, and the revival of international organisation. Conferences were called by the Committee for International Workers' Sport: in Paris (1945), Brussels (1946) and Warsaw (1947). The BWSA resumed its international connection, but sadly the movement became a victim of cold war politics. In 1949 the international body refused to exclude Communists, and the BWSA withdrew under pressure from the Labour Party and TUC. British attempts to form a non-Communist grouping failed, and when the BWSA re-affiliated to the International in 1954 Labour and TUC financial support was stopped. The National Clarion maintained its support for the BWSA until it was wound up in 1960. But before this, the BWSA had donated a trophy which is still awarded annually to the Section claiming the highest aggregate distance actually cycled to the Easter Meet.

The Post-War Cycling Boom – and Slump

As with most other sports and pastimes, cycling benefited from a post-war boom after 1945 in both racing and touring. The Clarion's national membership rose from under 3,000 in 1944 to well over 6,000 in 1949 (nearly as many as in 1938). Its racing reputation had been enhanced in May 1944 when Cyril Cartwright of Manchester Clarion C. & A.C. became the first to complete a 25-mile time-trial in under an hour. (The course was based on the East Lancashire Road, and the time recorded was 59 minutes, 18 seconds.)

Enthusiasm for cycle-sport among Clarion members returning to civilian life after the war was high. The annual track meeting (the Manchester Sports) was revived at Fallowfield in 1947. Time-trialling became so popular that individual Sections of the National Clarion began to form their own C. & A.C. centres for racing purposes (instead of these being based on the regional Unions as in pre-war days). And in the late 1940s cycle touring reached a peak comparable with the 1930s, with dozens of riders on each of the Sunday club-runs organised by more than a hundred Clarion Sections up and down the country.

Sadly, however, these years were just an Indian summer for the Clarion. The time when cycling was a universally popular pastime and a part of everyday life for the mass of people was soon to end. By the end of the 1950s there were five times as many cars on the roads of Britain as there had been before the second world war. The shift towards a car-dominated society was reflected in the Clarion's membership figures. The fall was steady and relentless: under 5,000 by 1951, under 4,000 by 1953, under 3,000 by 1957, well under 2,000 by 1961, less than 1,000 in 1965 – and no more than 500 by the end of the 20th century.

It had always been a financial battle to keep the Clubhouses open, especially during the two world wars, but the changed conditions of the 1950s made their problems more acute. The programme for the 1950 Easter Meet at Buxton indicated that Ribble Valley, Menston, Valley

House and Dore were still open, but by 1960 only the Yorkshire Clarion Clubhouse at Menston was left. Valley House was closed and sold after the local council in Wilmslow stipulated that work costing £2,000 was needed to bring facilities up to the legally required standards of hygiene. The site was used to build an hotel convenient for nearby Manchester Airport. The Ribble Valley Clubhouse became a licensed restaurant, then a private residence. The truth was that the rising expectations of Clarion members about holiday accommodation and catering in a period of increasing 'affluence' could not be met without considerable investment. The Menston Clubhouse, which still offers hostel-type accommodation and camping facilities to Clarion members and others, has survived partly by using some of its land as a residential caravan site. But its continued existence owes much to the devotion, hard work and financial sacrifice of ordinary men and women. (This kind of dedication has also been responsible for the survival of Clarion House at Roughlee in Lancashire, now a tea-room for ramblers and cyclists, which was opened by Nelson ILP in 1912 and has been lovingly maintained by voluntary effort.)

Socialism Under Attack

Other cycling clubs and organisations also suffered a decline in membership as British society's love affair with the motor-car developed: but to a lesser extent, because the Clarion bore the extra burden of attacks on Socialism in the 1950s. It was the era of cold war panic about the spread of Russian-style Communism, and Socialists of all kinds were suspected of being 'fellow-travellers' with the Stalinists. The humanistic and libertarian Socialism of the Clarion's early decades was very far removed from the ideologies of oppressive and authoritarian East European regimes, but the mass media tarred all Socialists with the same brush. And just as some Labour Party politicians began to fight shy of using a word embodying the principles which to their predecessors were the 'hope of the world', so in the National Clarion did some of the politically-committed begin to give way in the face of mounting criticism of the Socialist connection.

There had never been any attempt to exclude non-Socialists, or even anti-Socialists, from membership of the Clarion organisations – even in the pre-1914 years of political activism. On the contrary, it was thought that those who joined as non-Socialists might eventually be converted by contact with the practice of Morris's 'good fellowship' and Kropotkin's 'mutual aid'. But there had always been critics within the

Clarion membership who, in today's terms, did not see why politics and sport should be mixed, and who pressed for the link with Socialism to be severed.

Socialist propaganda had been included as a principal object in the NCCC constitution right from the start in 1895, but it had been left to individual local clubs to ensure, if members so wished, that their elected officials were Socialists. In the early years of the century many members wanted such a restriction to be included in the national rules. At the 1904 Easter Meet in Nantwich it was agreed to recommend to local clubs that officials be 'avowed' Socialists, but not necessarily members of a Socialist organisation, since this was seen as difficult to define.

When a new Constitution and Rules were drawn up in 1905 by a National Committee meeting at the Handforth Clubhouse, the objects were stated for the first time as "Mutual Aid, Good Fellowship and the Propagation of the Principles of Socialism as advocated by the *Clarion*." The first national membership cards in 1906 had these words printed on the front. This practice continued into the 1930s, except that the reference to the paper was cut out in 1918 following angry opposition to the pro-war policy of Blatchford and his fellow-editors. The key words remained in the 1995 Constitution and Rules as the objects of the NCCC, although the words "propagation of" were replaced by "support for".

The rule that the national officials and committee should be Socialists also survived (on paper at least), though over the years the wording fluctuated between "members of a Socialist organisation" and merely "declared" or "avowed" Socialists. Attempts at a definition, however, by giving a list of examples (e.g. Labour Party, ILP, Communist Party, or member of an affiliated Trade Union) were abandoned.

Though political propaganda by Clarion Sections declined in the inter-war years, to the consternation of both older members like Tom Groom and younger activists, the practice of having Socialist speakers at Easter Meet public meetings continued well into the 1930s. And the words of the Internationale were printed in successive annual editions of the NCCC Handbook between 1932 and 1938.

In 1939, after national membership had fallen by about 2,000 over a two-year period, some blamed left-wing politics for the drop. A member's letter printed in the London Union's magazine *Boots* gives an indication of the controversy which resulted:

> True, our membership has declined, but what is the real cause? In my opinion it is because the club is wobbling between a policy of:

'let's be really political', and 'don't let's touch politics.' Let us come down on one side or the other. If it is to be the latter we can be sure that most political members left would consider that they were wasting their time and join other organisations. The Clarion would become just another cycling club. I am convinced however that if a definite stand were taken on the former position we could draw many new recruits into our ranks. If the Clarion of 1900 did it, then it should be possible for us to do it. I know the conditions were different then – but it was they who had the more difficult task, not us.

That year at the Annual Conference in York, attempts were made to eliminate references to Socialism in the Constitution and Rules. The London Union submitted a resolution which would have struck out "propagation of the principles of Socialism" from the objects. The South Wales Union wanted to remove the "members of a Socialist organisation" qualification for officials and National Committee members. The London resolution was lost, causing the one from South Wales to be withdrawn. But after the war attempts like this were taken up again by a growing minority within the Clarion, especially in the 1950s.

At the Great Malvern Easter Meet in 1951, against the background of the Korean War and an 'anti-Red' cold-war offensive in Britain and the USA, the Communist Party was deleted from the list of examples of Socialist organisations in the rules (by a two-vote majority!) But a year later, attempts to remove the Socialist qualification for national officials and committee were defeated.

In 1954 Ernest Sugden (a Labour Alderman in Halifax) retired from the position of National Clarion Secretary at the age of seventy, after 33 years in the job (full-time and paid in the 1930s). He had joined the Clarion in 1902. In his last Annual Report he wrote:

One of the objects of our Club is the propagation of the principles of Socialism, and this is reflected in our rules, our membership forms and our notepaper. It is not, however, reflected in our activities, and only our older members can recall the days when the Clarion Cycling Club was active in the political sphere. There is no road back to the propaganda drives of the past, but it is only if we keep our Club's history in mind that we have a right to call ourselves the Clarion Cycling Club. We all know that the Club was formed by a band of men imbued with the spirit of Socialism, who cycled out into the countryside every week to distribute pamphlets, hold meetings and try in every way to spread their ideas. Socialists and cyclists, they decided to form a club that was different from all the others springing up at that time. With their motto 'Fellowship is Life' they attracted towards them an ever-growing number of Socialist cyclists, and they built up a club which became a byword ... Times have changed and we do not wish to live in days gone by, but our fore-runners who believed as we believe that 'Socialism is the Hope of the World' made our Club great in the past. They left us a great tradition which we cannot afford to forget.

The Annual Conference at York which received Sugden's last report rejected a resolution from Ossett and Horbury Section which demanded that all political propaganda be removed from Club literature and that "all political rules be severed from the organisation."

Joe Rigby, who took over from Ernest Sugden as National Secretary, tried to respond to opponents of the Clarion's Socialist basis in the 1955 Handbook:

With monotonous regularity over the last few years we have been asked at our Annual Conference why we persist in continuing an association which no longer appears to hold any meaning. The answer is, in my opinion, (and I know it is the opinion of many of our members) that as a cycling club we should stand by our belief in Socialism, not because we want our members to talk politics but (so that) we have a common bond between us. Our members can propagate their principles in their conduct in the club and, if they wish to do so in a more active manner, there are ample opportunities outside of cycling club activities. We cannot expect or insist that our younger members have any political opinions, but if by the example of our older members we can demonstrate that our Clarion motto of 'Fellowship Is Life' is a living thing there can be no doubt that we shall be helping to maintain the tradition which the pioneers of our Club worked for.

The debate continued at the 1955 Easter Meet in Peterborough when an anti-Socialist (though not anti-Labour Party) resolution was lost by 135 to 137 votes. The following year's Conference in Mablethorpe approved a resolution from Ossett & Horbury and Peterborough Sections that shares in the Communist *Daily Worker* be disposed of. And Tom Groom's heritage received a blow in 1957 when it was decided that in future the question in the claim form for the trophy bearing his name which asked "Has your Section organised any political meetings?" should be omitted since it appeared to be redundant.

The dwindling number of members with a Socialist commitment fought a dogged rearguard action. Marian Lamb, who edited the Manchester Union's duplicated magazine *The Trumpet* in the 1950s, and who later was to be National Secretary for 25 years from 1966 to 1991, quoted (in May 1956) from a *Manchester Union Handbook* for 1915, and commented:

Happy days? In many aspects, yes! But the 'old brigade' were of the pioneering kind who helped to create the benefits you now enjoy and who were not afraid of hard work or the Socialist 'Bogey' that seems to haunt some of our present-day members. It would indeed be wonderful if we could recapture the fighting spirit of the Comrades of those days and if we could equal the Manchester Union's 1915 membership of 2,000 Socialists!

(Sadly, the regional Unions had completely disappeared by the 1970s.)

Willie Pollock of Glasgow, one-time Secretary of the Scottish Union and for many years a greatly-respected National Committee member, wrote in the September 1963 issue of the NCCC Gazette about the Socialism of William Morris and Robert Blatchford, and their belief that there should be a life outside the serious concerns of political activism. In Willie's words: "Socialists of the Clarion believe that we have a duty to ourselves and to our Socialist ideals to help all people to know and to enjoy life to the full."

Jim Straker of Leeds, Secretary of the Yorkshire Union and National Committee member from the 1950s to the 1970s, was another who held with Tom Groom that Socialism was the life-blood of the National Clarion CC. In September 1970, with membership down to below 800, he maintained in a piece he wrote for another short-lived NCCC magazine *Boots! Spurs!* that, "numbers are not all".

"I joined the Clarion," he went on, "purely because of the principles on which it was founded." In those days, "all accepted the belief that colour, creed, race and religion, or money, were incidentals; and all realised that life meant more than just riding a bike." Where Sections were only cycling clubs, there was, he suggested "a decline in the desire to meet up with and mix with other Sections".

Jim had fears about the Clarion's future. "The very idea," he declared, "that at some future Meet a Quintin Hogg [a leading Tory politician] or like person, might be invited to present the Tom Groom, British Workers' Sports Association and Czechoslovakia trophies would make me physically sick."

Despite these brave voices, Socialism was on the retreat in what was left of the Clarion movement. Walter Crane's 1912 letterhead with its figure of a young woman representing Socialism came to be known by some as the 'Flying Angel', and its inscription "Socialism the Hope of the World"' was changed. It now read "The Club for Wise Cyclists", so as not to frighten away potential sponsors or members.

In 1995 the objects of the Club as printed in the Constitution and Rules – "Mutual Aid, Good Fellowship and support for the Principles of Socialism" – would have won the approval of the pioneers of 1895. These words retained their precarious place in spite of repeated attempts to delete them. Yet even the existing slender connection with Socialism seemed likely to vanish when the few remaining old-timers had faded from the scene. Already the rule which required that National Committee members and officials should be members of a Socialist organisation had to be ignored because so few would qualify.

Nevertheless, on 26th February 1994, with eighteen Sections remaining and a national membership of around 600, a celebration lunch was held in Birmingham, exactly one hundred years to the day after the inaugural meeting of the first Clarion Cycling Club. And on the May Day week-end a Centenary Ride for vintage machines took eighteen brave cyclists, led by Merlin Evans of Stockport Clarion, from Birmingham to Manchester via Ashbourne, finishing at the newly-opened People's History Museum with its Clarion Cafe.

Easter 1995 saw the 100th Annual Meet at Skegness, attracting no more than the number of Clarionettes which attended the first one at Ashbourne in 1895 – but with a higher proportion of girls and women, and a wider age-range, from toddlers to octogenarians. There was the same good fellowship – even mutual aid – but what had dimmed for many was the belief that Socialism would be the 'hope of the world' in the next century.

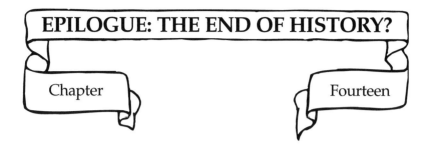

EPILOGUE: THE END OF HISTORY?

Chapter   Fourteen

Though Socialism was fading within the National Clarion in the 1970s, there was at the same time in Britain a revival of interest in cycling as part of a modest reaction against the car-worshipping culture established in the 1950s and 60s. Richard Ballantine's best-selling *Bicycle Book*, first published here in 1975, signalled the start of a slow change in public attitudes. He claimed advantages for the bicycle on grounds of economy and convenience, as well as fitness and health; but he also pointed to the urgent necessity of combatting environmental pollution caused by over-reliance on motor transport. Writing approvingly of a massive 1972 anti-car demonstration in Paris, involving thousands of bicycles, and supported by Friends of the Earth, public transport users and Socialists, he called for the "absolute elimination of internal combustion engines from urban areas". "Present transport systems," he added, "are filling the air with deadly fumes and noise, and recklessly wasting a dwindling supply of natural resources." He advocated putting pressure on local and central government planners to make special provision for cyclists.

For Ballantine the car was an enemy, "a tool with a backlash of millions of dead and grievously injured". In contrast, he cited Ivan Illich's praise for the bicycle as a "tool for conviviality" (a word which comes close to what William Morris and the Clarion cyclists had meant by 'fellowship'). Illich had underlined the connection between bikes and social equality when he wrote: "Socialism will only come, riding on a bicycle."

Pressure by environmentalists on an international scale over the last thirty years has led to the wide recognition of an urgent need to promote non-polluting forms of transport. Central government in Britain started to direct local planning authorities to "promote acceptable alternatives to the private car", and to "encourage the implementation of specific measures to assist people to use bicycles". (*Department of Environment and Department of Transport Planning Policy Guidance*, No.13, 1994.)

The future of cycling seemed to be assured into the 21st century, but what about Socialism? By the late 1980s it was fashionable, even among some people who had previously been on the left politically, to say that Socialism was dead. According to some, the overthrow of Communist regimes in the USSR and Eastern Europe had brought about the 'end of history' and the triumph of capitalist liberal democracy. In Britain the leadership of the Labour Party had long since ceased to pay even lip-service to the Socialist objective of common ownership and control of the means of production and distribution, and it was eventually written out of the party's constitution.

But although the word Socialism has been misused and rejected, many still hold dear the ideal that wealth should be shared according to need in a society based on voluntary co-operation between equals. The word may have been corrupted and deliberately misrepresented, but belief in the principles behind it are still very much alive. Evidence of this can be seen in the support, especially among young people, for campaigns against racism, the poll tax, motorway construction, and capitalist globalization.

There will be cycling Socialists through the 21st century, as there were throughout the 20th, but whether the Clarion Cycling Club will survive in its present form to attract their support remains to be seen. Remembering the work of pioneers like Tom Groom, we may hope so, yet it is not the names of organisations and movements which are important, but the principles which their members hold and practise.

William Morris still speaks to us, as he did to Socialists over a century ago in *A Dream of John Ball*, when he reflected on:

... how men fight and lose the battle, and the thing they fought for comes about in spite of their defeat, and when it comes turns out not to be what they meant, and other men have to fight for what they meant under another name ...

He speaks to us also in a passage containing the words which for more than a century have inspired Clarion men and women:

... fellowship is heaven, and lack of fellowship is hell: fellowship is life, and lack of fellowship is death: and the deeds that ye do upon the earth, it is for fellowship's sake that ye do them, and the life that is in it, that shall live on and on for ever, and each one of you part of it ...

BIBLIOGRAPHY AND REFERENCES

Ballantine, Richard, *Richard's Bicycle Book*, Pan, 1975.

Beckett, Alf, Letters (1956) in possession of Derek Roberts, Editor, *Fellowship News* (Fellowship of Cycling Old-Timers).

Bellamy, J.M., & Saville, J., *Dictionary of Labour Biography*, Macmillan, 1972-.

Bird, Stephen, 'The British Workers' Sports Association, 1930-1960', *Bulletin of the Society for the Study of Labour History*, No.50, 1985.

Blatchford, Robert, *Merrie England*, Clarion Office/Walter Scott, 1893.

Blatchford, Robert, *My Eighty Years*, Cassell, 1931.

Coates, Collin, Letters (1968-1977) in possession of Derek Roberts, Editor, *Fellowship News* (Fellowship of Cycling Old-Timers).

Eastwood, Jack, articles and letters in *Bolton Evening News*, (Sports Edition), early 1900s to 1920s.

Fincher, Judith, 'The Clarion Movement 1891-1914', MA Thesis, Manchester University, 1971.

Goode, Christopher, 'The Clarion, Cycling and Nascent Socialism', BA Dissertation, Manchester Polytechnic, 1990.

Groom, Tom, *The National Clarion Cycling Club 1894-1944*, Jubilee Souvenir, NCCC, 1944.

Illich, Ivan, *Tools for Conviviality*, Fontana, 1975.

Jones, Leslie, *Robert Blatchford and the Clarion*, Hyde Park Pamphlet No.9, London, no date.

Liddington, Jill & Norris, Jill, *One Hand Tied Behind Us*, Virago, 1978.

Lyons, Neil, *Robert Blatchford*, Clarion Press, 1910.

Nally, Michael, 'The Dear Old Perisher – The *Clarion* Newspaper 1891-1935' *North West Labour History*, No.17, 1992/93.

Pearce, Georgia (ed.), *The Clarion Song Book*, Clarion Press, 1906.

Prynn, David, 'The Clarion Clubs, Rambling and the Holiday Associations in Britain since the 1890s', *Journal of Contemporary History*, Vol.II, 1976.

Pye, Denis, 'The Manchester Clarion Clubhouses 1897-1951', *North West Labour History*, No.17, 1992/93.

Pye, Denis, 'Socialism, Fellowship and Food': Manchester's Clarion Café 1908-1936' *North West Labour History*, No.21, 1996/97.

Thompson, Alex. M., *Here I Lie*, Routledge, 1937.

Thompson, Laurence, *Robert Blatchford: Portrait of an Englishman*, Gollancz, 1951.

ARCHIVES

Manchester Central Library Local Studies Unit (Archives Section): Clarion Collection (Calendars & Lists, Reference 016); National Museum of Labour History, Archive & Study Centre, Manchester: *Clarion* newspaper files, and Clarion Collection; Working Class Movement Library, Salford: Clarion pamphlets, etc.

NEWSPAPERS & MAGAZINES

Boots (London & Southern Counties Union, 1939), *Boots–Spurs: NCCC Gazette* (1969-71), *The Clarion* (1891-1932),*The Clarion Cyclist* (1930-31, 1936-37), *The Clarion Cyclists' Journal* (1896-98), *King of the Road* (1897), *NCCC Gazette* (1963-65), *The Scout: A Journal for Socialist Workers* (1895-96), *The Trumpet: Journal of the Manchester Union* (1943-56).

APPENDIX I
National Clarion Cycling Club Easter Meets

1st	1895 Ashbourne	37th	1932 York	73rd	1968 Scarborough
2nd	1896 Bakewell	38th	1933 Nottingham	74th	1969 Great Malvern
3rd	1897 Leek	39th	1934 Lincoln	75th	1970 Southport
4th	1898 Chester	40th	1935 Shrewsbury	76th	1971 Skegness
5th	1899 Skipton	41st	1936 Chester	77th	1972 Skegness
6th	1900 Shrewsbury	42nd	1937 Durham	78th	1973 Scarborough
7th	1901 Bakewell	43rd	1938 Gloucester	79th	1974 Blackpool
8th	1902 Stafford	44th	1939 York	80th	1975 Cleethorpes
9th	1903 Chester	45th	1940 Buxton	81st	1976 Bridlington
10th	1904 Nantwich	46th	1941 Valley House	82nd	1977 Skegness
11th	1905 Worksop		(Styal)	83rd	1978 Fleetwood
12th	1906 Warwick	47th	1942 Leicester	84th	1979 Cleethorpes
13th	1907 Matlock	48th	1943 York	85th	1980 Fleetwood
14th	1908 Shrewsbury	49th	1944 Buxton	86th	1981 Skegness
15th	1909 Lincoln	50th	1945 Leamington	87th	1982 Morecambe
16th	1910 Chester	51st	1946 Chester	88th	1983 Whitby
17th	1911 Warwick	52nd	1947 Cheltenham	89th	1984 Llandudno
18th	1912 Buxton	53rd	1948 Edinburgh	90th	1985 Cleethorpes
19th	1913 York	54th	1949 Shrewsbury	91st	1986 Fleetwood
20th	1914 Shrewsbury	55th	1950 Buxton	92nd	1987 Skegness
21st	1915 Buxton	56th	1951 Durham	93rd	1988 Morecambe
22nd	1916 Crewe	57th	1952 Great Malvern	94th	1989 Scarborough
23rd	1917 Buxton	58th	1953 Shrewsbury	95th	1990 Blackpool
	1918 No Meet	59th	1954 York	96th	1991 Skegness
24th	1919 Leamington	60th	1955 Peterborough	97th	1992 Llandudno
25th	1920 York	61st	1956 Mablethorpe	98th	1993 Whitby
26th	1921 Chester	62nd	1957 Harrogate	99th	1994 Lincoln
27th	1922 Shrewsbury	63rd	1958 Great Malvern	100th	1995 Skegness
28th	1923 Buxton	64th	1959 Buxton	101st	1996 Llandudno
29th	1924 Warwick	65th	1960 York	102nd	1997 Whitby
30th	1925 Chester	66th	1961 Great Malvern	103rd	1998 Torquay
31st	1926 Lincoln	67th	1962 Skegness	104th	1999 Bangor
32nd	1927 York	68th	1963 Morecambe	105th	2000 Skegness
33rd	1928 Shrewsbury	69th	1964 Skegness	106th	2001 Llandudno
34th	1929 Chester	70th	1965 Buxton	107th	2002 Whitby
35th	1930 Buxton	71st	1966 Southport	108th	2003 Morecambe
36th	1931 Warwick	72nd	1967 New Brighton	109th	2004 Scarborough

APPENDIX II
Clarion Cycling Club National Secretaries

1899-1904	J. Taylor Clark (Stalybridge)
1904-1906	John Pownall-Goodhall (Manchester)
1906	Will Booker & Alf Short (Sheffield)
1906-1907	Tom Stanley & Fred Farrand (Leeds)
1907-1911	Tom Stanley (Leeds)
1911-1916	Tom Groom (Gloucester & Kidderminster)
1916-1921	Tom Stevens (Birmingham)
1921-1954	Ernest Sugden (Halifax)
1954-1958	Joe Rigby (Stockport)
1958-1959	Basil Kite (London)
1959-1964	Lil Dumbell (Stockport)
1965	Muriel Ames (Gateshead)
1966-1991	Marian Lamb (Manchester & Wilmslow)
1991-1999	Ian Clarke (Peterborough)
1999-2003	Frank Bibby (Bolton)
2003-	Charles Jepson (Blackburn)

INDEX

Amateur Athletics Association (AAA) 72-3
Ancoats (Manchester) 6, 42
Ashbourne News 17
Atkinson, Harry ('McAtkinson') 9, 17, 19, 33

Badges, Clarion 10, 15, 17, 49, 53
Band, Liverpool Socialist 38, 49
Belle Vue (Manchester)62-3, 65
Bell's Life 5
Bennett, George 69
Blatchford, Corri 57
Blatchford, Montague ('Mont Blong') 4, 15, 17, 19-20, 28, 43, 49
Blatchford, Robert ('Nunquam') 3-8, 15, 19, 20-3, 27-8, 30-2, 36, 41, 43, 47, 54-8
Blatchford, Sarah (Sally) 5, 57
Blatchford, Winifred 5, 54
Board, The (of the *Clarion* paper) 7, 8, 15, 38, 40, 42, 49, 58
Bolton Evening News 87
'Boots! Spurs!' (Clarion greeting and response) 15, 38, 77
Boughton, Rutland 50
'Bounder, The' (see Fay, Edward Francis)
British Socialist Party (BSP) 55
British Workers' Sports Association

(BWSA) 72-4, 77-8
British Workers' Sports Federation (BWSF) 68-71
Brockway, Fenner 56
Browne, FG 14

C. & A.C.s (Clarion Cycling & Athletic Clubs) 64-5, 78
West of Scotland 74
Cafes, Clarion
Liverpool 53
Manchester 53, 84
Camera Club, Clarion 52
camps, Clarion
Tabley Brook 37, 42-3
Bradford Clarion 46
Sheffield Clarion 60
Cartwright, Cyril 78
Celtic Park (Glasgow) 63
choirs, Socialist (see Vocal Unions, Clarion)
Cinderella Clubs 11, 21, 43, 52, 63
Clarion, The (newspaper) 6-16, 18, 21-2, 25-8, 30, 32, 35-9, 42-3, 47-50, 53-60, 62, 65, 67-8, 80, 87
Clarion Cycling Clubs (see Sections, of National Clarion CC)

Clarion Cyclist (monthly) 70-1
Clark, J.Taylor ('JTC' or 'Jatece') 23-4, 40
Clubhouses, Clarion Cyclists'
  Liverpool
    Burton 61
    Halewood 47
    London (Nazeing, Essex) 47
  Manchester
    Bucklow Hill 43-4
    Handforth 3, 44-6, 52, 61, 64, 80
    Valley House 61, 76, 78-9
  Midlands
    Sheldon 60-1
    Yardley 47
  Ribble Valley 46-7, 61, 78
  Roughlee (Nelson ILP) 79
  Sheffield (Dore Moor) 60, 79
  South East Lancashire (Tottington) 60-1
  Yorkshire (Chevin End, Menston) 46, 61,
    72, 78
Clubs, Clarion Cycling (see Sections,
  of National Clarion CC)
Communist Party 57, 69, 77, 79-82
Constitution & Rules (of National Clarion
  CC) 26, 57, 80-2
Cox, Roy 73
Crane, Walter 20, 25, 41, 53, 84
Cyclists' Touring Club (CTC) 26, 70-1

Daily Herald 72
'Dangle' (see Thompson, AM)
Dawson, Julia (Mrs DJ Myddleton-Worrall)
  36-7, 40
Derbyshire Times 20
Deveney, Ernest 70
Deveney, Jack 69-70
Dramatic Societies, Clarion 51-2
Durban, Tom 73

Easter Meets (see Meets, Annual)
Eastwood, Jack ('JWE') 59
Edwards, John 38
Esperanto 67
Evans, Merlin 84

Fallowfield track (Manchester) 65, 78
Fay, Edward Francis ('The Bounder') 5,
  10-2, 15, 48
Fellowship, Clarion 53
Field Clubs, Clarion 50-1
  London 50-1

Ghent Congress (1913) of Socialist Physical
  Education Groups 66

Grayson, Victor 55
Groom, Tom ('The O'Groomio') 4, 9-13,
  16-7, 19-21, 23-4, 26, 33, 38, 43, 47, 55-6,
  60-1, 63-4, 66-9, 75-7, 82, 86
  Memorial Trophy 77, 82
Groom, Nancy 66
Grundy, Bill 74

Hagger, Fred 41, 66
Halifax 4-5, 15, 49, 81
Hall, Leonard 16
Hamilton, Gilbert 65
Handicraft Guilds, Clarion 24, 52
Hardie, Keir 2, 49, 54
Hartley, Edward R 40
Heath, Eric 74
Hirst, Tommy 64, 70
Holst, Gustav 49-50
Hore, T 24
Hulme (Manchester) 6
Hulton, Edward 5-6
Humphreys, Kenneth 64
Hyndman, HM 2, 6, 67

Ibrox stadium (Glasgow) 63
Independent Labour Party (ILP) 2, 16, 18,
  28, 32, 39-42, 68, 79-80
International Brigade 73-75
International, 'Red' Sports 69-70
International Socialist Sports Federation 66
International Union for Workers' Physical
  Education and Sport 67
International Workers' Sport, Committee
  for 77
International Workers' Sports Federation 66

Keeling, Eleanor 35
Kropotkin, Peter 79
'Kuklos' (Fitzwalter Wray) 72

Labour Churches 2, 9, 11
Labour Party 68-9, 77-8, 80-2, 86
Labour Sports Federation (France) 67
Lamb, Harold 75-6
Lamb, Marian 83
Land Restoration League 13, 36-7
Leeming, Frank ('Swiftsure') 12, 14-5, 35
Leeming, Mrs 63
Levy, Joseph 29
London 4-5, 8, 11, 25, 28, 40-1, 50-1, 55, 59,
  66, 68
London Evening News 17
London Labour Sports Association 69
'Lone Scout' (see Manson, Bob)

Lowerison, Harry 50, 55
Lucerne Congress (1920) (of International
 Workers' Sports Federation) 67, 69-71, 73

MacDonald, Ramsay 54, 60
Manchester 5-6, 15-16, 23, 25, 31-2, 34,
 42-4, 49, 65, 79, 84
Mann, Tom 31
Manson, Bob ('The Lone Scout', or
 'Manzona') 15, 21-2, 37-9, 54
Martyn, Caroline 37, 39-40, 49
Meets, Annual Easter (incl. NCCC
 Ann. Conferences –for complete list
 see Appendix I)
Ashbourne 1895 14-7
Bakewell 1896 18-20
 1901 24, 53
Buxton 1912 57
 1923 67-8
 1930 64, 70
 1940 75
 1944 76
 1950 78
Chester 1898 22-3
 1903 24-5
 1910 25, 55
 1921 67
 1929 64
 1936 72
Durham 1937 73
Gloucester 1938 74
Great Malvern 1951 81
Leek 1897 20-2
Mablethorpe 1956 82
Nottingham 1933 64
Peterborough 1955 82
Shrewsbury 1900 23-4
 1914 25-6, 41
 1922 64
 1928 64
 1935 65
Skegness 1995 84
Skipton 1899 23
Stafford 1902 24
Warwick 1911 25
 1931 70
York 1913 40
 1939 74-5
 1954 82
Meets, Scottish 24
Meets, Whitsun 18, 24
membership (National Clarion CC) 25, 58,
 60, 76, 78, 80-1, 84
Merrie England 27-8, 30, 33, 54

'Mont Blong' (see Blatchford, Montague)
Morris, William 2, 6, 17, 20, 31, 40, 43, 48,
 50, 53, 80, 85-6
Mowat, W 74
Muir, Steve 9
Mullineux, Jack 74

National Clarion Cycling Club (NCCC)
 formation of 15-8
 centenary of 84
National Clarion Cycling Friendly Society 26
National Committee (of Clarion CC) 18,
 20-6, 40, 57, 64, 66, 70, 72, 74-5, 80-1, 83-4
National Cyclists' Union (NCU) 62, 73-4
National Workers' Sports Association 69-70,
 72
New Leader (ILP paper) 68
Nield, Ada 37, 39
'Nunquam' (see Blatchford, Robert)

O'Donnell, Joe 38-9
O'Donnell, Will 38
'O'Groomio, The' (see Groom, Tom)
Olympiads, Workers' (also see
 Spartakiade, Workers')
Antwerp 1937 (3rd International) 73-4
Barcelona 1936 (People's) 72
Frankfurt 1925 (1st International) 68
Prague 1921 68
 1927 68
Rotterdam 1938 74
Vienna 1931 (2nd international) 69-70
Olympic Games, Berlin 1936 72-3
Ordinary bicycle ('penny-farthing') 1, 10, 19

Palmer, William ('Whiffly Puncto') 5, 15,
 19, 52
Peacock, W Arthur 57
'penny-farthing' (see Ordinary bicycle)
People's History Museum, Manchester 84
Pollock, Willie 83
Poole, George 25
Powell, W 9-10

Rambling Clubs, Clarion (also see
 Field Clubs)
Derby 51
Sheffield 51
Ranstead, William ('Candid Friend') 17, 19,
 28, 37-8, 42
rational dress (for women cyclists) 35-6
Reddish, Sarah 37
Reekie, Charlie ('O'Reekie' or
 'Auld Reekie') 14, 19, 42-3

ribbons, Easter Meet 25
Richards, J Cruwys 9, 52
Rigby, Joe 82
Roads Racing Council (RRC) 65
Road Time Trials Council (RTTC) 65
Rudge-Whitworth (cycle manufacturers) 63

Safety bicycle 1-2
Scout, The (A Journal for Socialist Workers)
28-31, 50
Scouts, Clarion 16, 27-30
Sections (of National Clarion CC –
Clarion Cycling Clubs until 1906)
Aston 74
Barnoldswick 69
Barnsley 12
Birmingham 9-17, 22, 27, 33, 38, 48, 62, 64
Blackburn 14, 64, 70
Bolton 21, 36, 59, 64, 74
Bradford 12, 14, 28, 46
Bristol 19, 21, 33
Burnley 14, 57
Crewe 57
Darlington 32
Glasgow 33, 57, 63, 65, 72
Hyde 14
Leeds 14
Leicester 77
Lincoln 74
Liverpool 12, 15, 17, 21, 27-8, 30, 32, 38,
54, 61
London (South East) 64
Manchester 14-5, 17-8, 32, 34, 57, 62
Nelson 14
Newcastle-on-Tyne 14, 37
Nottingham 14-5, 18, 63
Oldham 63, 70
Portsmouth 33
Potteries (Hanley) 12, 15, 27-8, 48, 62
Springburn (Glasgow) 65
Stockport 63, 84
Stretford 75-6
Wigan 14
Wolverhampton 38
Sexton, Jimmy 17
Social Democratic Federation (SDF) 2, 10,
16, 28, 55
Socialist Sports Federation (France) 66
Southgate, Walter 25
Spanish Medical Aid Committee 73
Spartakiade, Workers'
Moscow 1928 69
Berlin 1931 70
Straker, Jim 83

Sugden, Ernest 68, 70, 75, 81-2
Sunday Chronicle 5-6
Sutcliffe, JD ('The Cheery One') 17, 23, 42
Suthers, Robert 6
'Swiftsure' (see Leeming, Frank)

Taylor, Alex 65, 74
Taylor, Jack 65, 72, 74
Thompson, Alex M ('Dangle') 5, 15-7, 19,
22, 25, 32, 38, 43, 55-8
Thompson, Chris 9-10
Tillett, Ben 14
time-trials 63-5, 71, 74, 78
Trades Union Congress (TUC) 65, 69, 77-8
Trumpet, The (Manchester Union
magazine) 76-7, 83

Unions (of Clarion CC Sections) 25-6
Birmingham 25
London 25, 69, 80-1
Manchester 25, 41, 45, 64, 76, 83
Midlands, North 26
Midlands, South 26
North Lancashire 25, 41, 46, 60
Scottish 25, 41
Southern Counties 26, 73
South West Lancs & Cheshire 26
Western Counties 26
Yorkshire 26, 41, 60, 83

Vans, Clarion 34, 36-41, 59-60
'Caroline Martyn' Memorial (No.1) 39-40
'EF Fay' 40
'Enid Stacy' 40
Glasgow Handicraft Guild 41
Pioneer (Women's) 37-40, 42
'William Morris' 40
Van, Red (of the English Land Restoration
League) 13, 36-7
Van, Yellow (of the Land Nationalisation
Society) 37
Veitch, Norman 52
Vocal Unions, Clarion (CVUs) 40, 48-9
Halifax 49
Meet (Hardcastle Crags) 49, 59

Waddington, Joe ('Clarion Joe') 6, 8
'Whiffly Puncto' (see Palmer, William)
White, Tom 76
White, Walter 10
women (and cycling) 11, 34-6
Wray, Fitzwalter (see 'Kuklos')

Yorkshireman, The 5